Business Miscellany

OTHER ECONOMIST BOOKS

Guide to Analysing Companies
Guide to Business Modelling
Guide to Business Planning
Guide to Economic Indicators
Guide to the European Union
Guide to Financial Markets
Guide to Investment Strategy
Guide to Management Ideas
Numbers Guide
Style Guide

Dictionary of Business
Dictionary of Economics
International Dictionary of Finance

Brands and Branding
Business Consulting
Business Strategy
China's Stockmarket
Economics
Future of Technology
Globalisation
Headhunters and How to Use Them
Mapping the Markets
The City
Wall Street

Essential Director
Essential Economics
Essential Investment
Essential Negotiation

Pocket World in Figures

Business Miscellany

THE ECONOMIST IN ASSOCIATION WITH
PROFILE BOOKS LTD

Published by Profile Books Ltd
3A Exmouth House, Pine Street, London EC1R 0JH
www.profilebooks.com

Designed by Sue Lamble and BRILL
Typeset by MacGuru Ltd
info@macguru.org.uk

Printed and bound in Great Britain by
Clays, Bungay, Suffolk

A CIP catalogue record for this book is available
from the British Library

ISBN-10: 1 86197 866 9
ISBN-13: 978 1 86197 866 0

Contents

Contributors

Many people contributed to this book, as follows.

Sarah Dallas, Cities Guide editor of Economist.com: "Business etiquette".

Tim Hindle, former management editor of *The Economist*: "Leading management thinkers", "Great business books" and "Business jargon".

Bob Tricker, author of *Essential Director*: "Games directors play".

Alexander Walsh, a freelance writer and researcher: "What companies say about themselves" and "Some business giants of the past".

Jonathan Williams and **Katie Eagleton** of the British Museum: "Some money superlatives".

Simon Wright, a member of Economist.com's Global Agenda team: "Behind the corporate name", "Business blunders", "Some famous advertising slogans", "Bubbles that burst", "Bad boys – and something fishy", "In their own words", "Behind the currency name" and "Inventors and inventions".

All other material was researched and compiled by Carol Howard, head of *The Economist* research department, Rishad Jonuschat and Christopher Wilson, with help from Andrea Burgess and Conrad Heine, all of whom work at *The Economist*.

❝ Business is really more agreeable than pleasure; it interests the whole mind ... more deeply. But it does not look as though it did **❞**

Walter Bagehot, journalist, author and, from 1861 to 1877, editor of *The Economist*

When firms ✸ *started*

Year	Firm	Activity	Country
578	Kongo Gumi	Construction	Japan
1288	Stora Enso	Paper	Finland
1385	Antinori	Wine and olive oil	Italy
1526	Fabbrica D'Armi Pietro Beretta	Firearms	Italy
1623	Zildjian	Cymbal makers	Turkey
1630	Kikkoman	Soy sauce	Japan
1630	Sumitomo	Conglomerate	Japan
1639	Hugel & Fils	Wine	France
1642	James Lock	Hatters	UK
1672	C. Hoare & Co	Banking	UK
1698	Berry Bros & Rudd	Wine merchants	UK
1734	Taittinger	Champagne	France
1739	William Clark	Linens	UK
1748	Villeroy & Boch	Tableware	Germany
1759	Wedgwood	China	UK
1761	Faber-Castell	Pencils	Germany
1783	Waterford	Glassware	Ireland
1786	Molson	Brewing	Canada
1802	Du Pont	Chemicals	US
1853	Levi Strauss	Clothing	US
1860	Anheuser-Busch	Beer	US
1862	Bacardi	Rum	Cuba
1867	Standard Oil	Oil	US
1886	Coca-Cola	Soft drinks	US
1892	General Electric	Electrical equipment	US
1896	Barclays	Banking	US
1901	US Steel	Steel	US
1903	Ford Motor	Automotive	US
1909	BP (originally Anglo-Persian Oil)	Oil	UK
1916	BMW	Motor engineering	Germany
1946	Sony	Consumer electronics	Japan
1955	McDonald's first restaurant	Fast food	US
1962	Wal-Mart's first store	Retailing	US
1971	Starbucks	Coffee shops	US
1975	Microsoft	Software	US
1977	Apple Computer	Computers	US
1998	Google	Internet	US

Sources: Company websites; *Centuries of Success* by William T. O'Hara; *Family Business* magazine

Oldest family firms

Year est.	Company	Business	Country
578	Kongo Gumi	Construction	Japan
718	Hoshi Ryokan	Innkeeping	Japan
1000	Château de Goulaine	Vineyard/museum/ butterfly collection	France
1000	Foneria Pontificia Marinelli	Bell foundry	Italy
1141	Barone Ricasoli	Wine and olive oil	Italy
1295	Barovier & Toso	Glassmaking	Italy
1304	Hotel Pilgrim Haus	Innkeeping	Germany
1326	Richard de Bas	Paper-making	France
1369	Torrini Firenze	Goldsmiths	Italy
1385	Antinori	Wine and olive oil	Italy
1438	Camuffo	Shipbuilding	Italy
1495	Baronnie de Coussergues	Wine	France
1500	Grazia Deruta	Ceramics	Italy
1526	Fabbrica D'Armi Pietro Beretta	Firearms	Italy
1530	William Prym	Copper, brass, haberdashery	Germany
1541	John Brooke & Sons	Woollens	England
1551	Codorniu	Wine	Spain
1552	Fonjallaz	Wine	Switzerland
1568	Von Poschinger Manufaktur	Glassmaking	Germany
1589	Wachsendustrie Fulda Adam Gies	Candles and wax figures	Germany
1590	Berenerg Bank	Banking	Germany
1591	R Durtnell & Sons	Construction	England
1595	J. P. Epping of Pippsvadr	Groceries	Germany
1596	Eduard Meier	Shoes	Germany
c1600	Toraya	Confectionery	Japan

Source: www.familybusinessmagazine.com/oldworld.html

Oldest newspapers still in circulation

Year est.	Title	Country
1645	Post och Inrikes Tidningar	Sweden
1656	Haarlems Dagblad	Netherlands
1664	La Gazzetta di Mantova	Italy
1665	The London Gazette	UK
1703	Wiener Zeitung	Austria
1705	Hildesheimer Allgemeiner Zeitung	Germany
1709	Worcester Journal	UK
1711	The Newcastle Journal	UK
1712	The Stamford Mercury	UK
1720	The Northampton Mercury	UK
1725	Hanauer Anzeiger	Germany
1734	Lloyd's List	UK
1737	The Belfast News-Letter	UK
1738	Feuille d'Avis de Neuchâtel	Switzerland
1740	Darmstaedter Tageblatt	Germany
1747	Press & Journal	UK
1749	Berlingske Tidende	Denmark
1750	Giessener Anzeiger	Germany
1752	Leeuwarder Courant	Netherlands
1754	The Yorkshire Post	UK
1755	La Gazzetta di Parma	Italy
1758	Provinciale Zeeuwse Courant	Netherlands
1758	Norrköpings Tidningar	Sweden
1761	Saarbrücker Zeitung	Germany
1761	Schaumburger Zeitung	Germany
1762	24 heures/Feuille d'Avis de Lausanne	Switzerland

Sources: World Association of Newspapers; companies

The business pre$$

Beginnings

The Economist	1843
Financial Times	1888
Wall Street Journal	1889
Forbes	1917
Barron's	1921
Harvard Business Review	1922
Time	1923
BusinessWeek	1929
Fortune	1930
Fast Company	1995

Circulation, paid copies per issue

	Europe	N America	Asia-Pacific	Total
BusinessWeek	97,428	947,606	80,492	1,164,095
The Economist	371,243	569,336	117,247	1,096,154
Financial Times	266,918	135,754	37,925	440,597
Forbes	na	965,868	na	971,199
Fortune	106,515	834,890	88,621	1,022,652
Harvard Business Review	40,448	163,690	23,528	241,258
Time	550,152	4,269,569	312,224	5,195,259
Wall Street Journal	86,636	2,120,382	80,543	2,329,536

Note: Latest geographical breakdown as at July 2006. Total includes other areas.
Source: Audit Bureau of Circulations

The world's **BIGGEST** firms

1993	Revenue, $bn
General Motors (US)	133.6
Ford Motor (US)	108.5
Exxon (US)	97.8
Royal Dutch Shell (Netherlands/UK)	95.1
Toyota (Japan)	85.3
Hitachi (Japan)	68.6
IBM (US)	62.7
Matsushita Electric Industrial Co. (Japan)	61.4
General Electric (US)	60.8
Daimler-Benz (Germany)	59.1
Mobil (US)	56.6
Nissan (Japan)	53.8
BP (UK)	52.5
Samsung (South Korea)	51.3
Philip Morris (US)	50.6
IRI (Italy)	50.5
Siemens (Germany)	50.4
Volkswagen (Germany)	46.3
Chrysler (US)	43.6
Toshiba (Japan)	42.9

Source: *Fortune*

2006*	Market capitalisation, $bn
Exxon Mobil (US)	371.6
General Electric (US)	362.5
Microsoft (US)	281.2
Citigroup (US)	238.9
BP (UK)	233.3
Bank of America (US)	211.7
Royal Dutch Shell (Netherlands/UK)	211.3
Wal-Mart (US)	196.9
Toyota Motor (Japan)	196.7
Gazprom (Russia)	196.3
HSBC (UK)	190.3

2005	Revenue, $bn
Exxon Mobil (US)	339.9
Wal-Mart (US)	315.7
Royal Dutch Shell (Netherlands/UK)	306.7
BP (UK)	267.6
General Motors (US)	192.6
Chevron Texaco (US)	189.5
DaimlerChrysler (Germany/US)	186.1
Toyota Motor (Japan)	185.8
Ford Motor (US)	177.2
ConocoPhillips (US)	166.7
General Electric (US)	157.2
Total (France)	152.4
ING Group (Netherlands)	138.2
Citigroup (US)	131.0
AXA (France)	129.8
Allianz (Germany)	121.4
Volkswagen (Germany)	118.4
Fortis (Belgium)	112.4
Crédit Agricole (France)	110.8
AIG (US)	108.9

Source: *Fortune*

2006*	Market capitalisation, $bn
Procter & Gamble (US)	189.6
Pfizer (US)	183.4
Johnson & Johnson (US)	176.2
Saudi Basic Industries (Saudi Arabia)	175.7
AIG (US)	171.6
Total (France)	162.8
Mitsubishi UFJ Financial (Japan)	156.3
GlaxoSmithKline (UK)	151.9
Altria (US)	147.9

*As of March 31st.
Source: *Financial Times*

America's **BIGGEST** firms

1955	Revenue, $bn	1965	Revenue, $bn	1975	Revenue, $bn
General Motors	9.82	General Motors	17.00	Exxon	42.06
Exxon	5.66	Exxon	10.81	General Motors	31.55
US Steel	3.25	Ford Motor	9.67	Ford Motor	23.62
General Electric	2.96	General Electric	4.94	Texaco	23.26
Esmark	2.51	Mobil	4.50	Mobil	18.93
Chrysler	2.07	Chrysler	4.29	Chevron	17.19
Armour	2.06	US Steel	4.08	Gulf Oil	16.46
Gulf Oil	1.71	Texaco	3.57	General Electric	13.41
Mobil	1.70	IBM	3.24	IBM	12.68
DuPont	1.69	Gulf Oil	3.17	ITT Industries	11.15

1985	Revenue, $bn	1995	Revenue, $bn	2005	Revenue, $bn
Exxon	90.85	General Motors	154.95	Exxon Mobil	339.90
General Motors	83.89	Ford Motor	128.44	Wal-Mart	315.70
Mobil	56.05	Exxon	101.46	General Motors	192.60
Ford Motor	52.37	Wal-Mart	83.41	Chevron Texaco	189.50
Chevron Texaco	47.33	AT&T	75.09	Ford Motor	177.20
IBM	45.94	General Electric	64.69	ConocoPhillips	166.70
DuPont	35.92	IBM	64.05	General Electric	157.20
AT&T	33.19	Mobil	59.62	Citigroup	131.00
General Electric	27.95	Sears Roebuck	54.56	AIG	108.90
Amoco	26.95	Altria Group	53.78	IBM	91.10

Source: *Fortune*

BIG firms, **BIG** facts

Airbus delivered 95 aircraft in 1990, Boeing 381. In 2000 Airbus delivered 311 against Boeing's 489. In 2005 Airbus delivered 378 and Boeing 290.

Coca-Cola products are sold in more than 200 countries, approximately 1.3 billion beverage servings per day.

Exxon Mobil produced 4.1m oil-equivalent barrels of oil and gas per day in 2005; BP produced 4m and Royal Dutch Shell 3.4m.

Fidelity Investments had $1.3 trillion in managed assets at the end of March 2006 and it administers a further $1.3 trillion.

General Motors had 12% of the US car market in 1921; overtook Ford Motor in 1929; reached over 50% in the early 1960s; and fell to 24% in the first half of 2006.

McDonald's has more than 30,000 local restaurants in 119 countries, serving nearly 50m customers a day.

Microsoft's sales went over $1m in 1978; over $1 billion in 1990; over $10 billion in 1997. Revenues were $44.3 billion in the fiscal year ending June 2006.

Starbucks is in over 11,000 locations in 37 countries; long-term target is 30,000 stores worldwide with at least 15,000 outside the US.

TTE, a joint venture between China's TCL and France's Thomson, has slipped from being the world's largest TV manufacturing company, but still sold 22m colour TV sets in 2005, just below LG and Samsung.

Wal-Mart Stores employs 1.8m associates worldwide in more than 6,500 stores. More than 176m customers visit the stores every week.

Sources: Company reports; press reports

Behind the corporate name

Behind the corporate name

Adidas The German sporting-goods firm is named after its founder Adolf (Adi) Dassler.

Adobe Named after the creek that ran past the houses of the American software firm's founders, John Warnock and Chuck Geschke.

Aldi Named after its founder, the Albrecht family, and discount: what it does.

Alfa Romeo Anonima Lombarda Fabbrica Automobili was taken over by Nicola Romeo in 1915. The first Alfa Romeo, the Torpedo 20–30hp, was made in 1920.

Amazon.com Jeff Bezos, the American online retailer's founder, originally wanted to call his firm Cadabra.com, as in abracadabra, until his lawyer advised him that it sounded too much like cadaver. So the company was renamed after the world's second-longest river, which not coincidentally also comes near the beginning of alphabetical lists.

> **...but it sounded too much like** cadaver, **so the company was renamed**

Amstrad The British electronics company is a contraction of Alan Michael Sugar Trading, named after its founder.

Apple Steve Jobs, one of the firm's co-founders, either sought enlightenment in the orchards of a Hare Krishna commune, or tried an experimental all-fruit diet, or wanted to make a tribute to the Beatles and their business arm, Apple Corp. Apple paid the Beatles a substantial out-of-court settlement to use the name and legal disputes continue. The Apple Macintosh is named after a popular variety of American apple, the McIntosh. McIntosh Laboratory, an audio equipment firm, was also paid off for the use of its name.

Asda The British supermarket chain, now owned by Wal-Mart, is a contraction of Associated Dairies.

Aston Martin The Aston Hill races near Birmingham, where the British car company was founded, provided the inspiration for the first half of the name. This was married to the surname of the company's founder, Lionel Martin.

Atari Derives from Go, a Japanese board game. Atari is when all an opponent's stones are threatened with capture.

Audi Founded in 1909 by August Horch, who took the name from the Latin translation of Horch, meaning "hark" in English from the imperative form of *audire*, "to hear".

B&Q The British DIY chain takes its name from the initials of its founders, Richard Block and David Quayle.

BASF The German chemicals firm name is taken from *Badische Anilin und Soda Fabrik*. The company began by producing aniline and soda in the German state of Baden.

BMW Bayerische Motoren Werke was founded in Munich in 1917, originally to construct aircraft engines. The German car company's logo is inspired by a rotating propeller.

Bridgestone The Japanese tyremaker is named after its founder, Shojiro Ishibashi, whose surname means "stone bridge".

❝ Ishibashi means stone bridge in Japanese ❞

Canon The Precision Optical Instruments Laboratory took its new identity from the name of its first camera, the Kwannon. It also represents Kannon, the Japanese name of the Buddhist bodhisattva of mercy.

Casio Derives from the name of its founder, Kashio Tadao.

behind the corporate name *continued*

Coca-Cola The name is derived from the coca leaves and kola nuts that were part of the original flavouring of the drink that was launched as a health tonic in 1885. The coca leaf, from which cocaine is produced, undoubtedly gave Coke a kick; the last traces were removed in 1929.

Daewoo Means "Great Universe" in Korean.

Danone The food firm began producing yogurt in Barcelona in 1919. It takes its name from the nickname of Daniel, the son of the founder, Isaac Carasso.

eBay Pierre Omidyar, founder of the online auction site, wanted to use the name of his internet consultancy, Echo Bay Technology Group. But Echo Bay Mines, a gold mining company, had registered the name already.

Fiat Società Anonima Fabbrica Italiana Automobili Torino was founded in 1899 in Turin.

Google The name, taken from the word googol, a vast number represented by 1 followed by 100 noughts, started as a boast about the amount of information the search engine would be able to cover.

Haribo The German confectioner derives its name from that of the founder and the home city of the company, Hans Riegel from Bonn.

Hasbro The American toy was founded by the Hassenfeld Brothers.

Hewlett-Packard Bill Hewlett and David Packard tossed a coin to decide whether the company they founded would be called Hewlett-Packard or Packard-Hewlett. Bill presumably won.

Ikea The Swedish budget furniture-maker was founded by Ingvar Kamprad whose family home was a farm called Elmtaryd, near the Swedish village of Agunnaryd.

Intel Bob Noyce and Gordon Moore had hoped to call their microchip company Moore Noyce. Improbably, a hotel chain of the same name had beaten them to it so they went for a conflation of integrated electronics.

Kodak Is called Kodak because George Eastman, the camera company's founder, thought that it sounded good.

Lego From a Danish phrase, *leg godt*, which means "play well". Although Lego also means "I construct" in Latin, the firm's name predates its introduction of construction bricks.

❝ From a Danish phrase which means "play well" ❞

Lycos *Lycosidae*, the family name of wolf spiders, provided the inspiration. These spiders are excellent hunters that run after prey instead of catching it in a web.

Mattel The American toymaker's marque is a combination of the names of its founders, Harold Matson and Elliot Handler.

Mercedes Benz The German car company founded by Gottlieb Daimler and Karl Benz took its forename from the daughter of an Austrian businessman, Emil Jellinek. In 1898 he began to sell and promote their cars to wealthy clients and in 1900 invested in the company to aid the development of a new engine called the Mercedes-Benz. Mercedes was both his daughter's name and the pseudonym he used when racing the cars.

Microsoft Bill Gates wanted a name that suggested the microcomputer software that he would manufacture. Micro-soft dropped its original hyphen and went on to rule the world.

Mitsubishi The Japanese conglomerate's name refers to its three-diamond logo. It is a combination of the words *mitsu*, meaning three, and *hishi*, meaning water chestnut, a word that denotes a diamond shape in Japanese.

behind the corporate name *continued*

Motorola The Galvin Manufacturing Company started making car radios in the 1950s. The suffix –ola was popular in America at the time (eg, Rockola jukeboxes, Victrola sound equipment) for suggesting high-quality audio reproduction. Motorola is intended to suggest sound in motion.

Nabisco The American food firm was known as the National Biscuit Company until 1971.

Nike The American sports-equipment company is named after the Greek goddess of victory.

Nikon The original name of the camera company was Nippon Kogaku, meaning "Japanese optical".

Nissan The company was earlier known by the name Nippon Sangyo, meaning "Japanese industry".

Nokia Named after a small town in Finland that was home to a successful pulp and paper company that later expanded into rubber goods before hitting on the idea that mobile phones could prove popular.

Oracle Larry Ellison, Ed Oates and Bob Miner were working for the CIA as consultants on a project codenamed Oracle. The project funding ended but the three decided to finish what they had begun and to keep the name for their software company. One of Oracle's first customers was the CIA.

Pepsi Brad's Drink, a concoction formulated by Caleb Bradham, a pharmacist, was renamed Pepsi-Cola in 1898 after the kola nuts used in the recipe and possibly to incorporate pepsin, an enzyme produced in the stomach that helps digestion.

Royal Dutch Shell Its origins go back to the Shell Transport and Trading Company. It was established by Samuel & Co as a business that sold sea shells to Victorian natural-history enthusiasts. Later, the company thought that there could be a market for oil, which it began to trade.

Saab Svenska Aeroplane Aktiebolaget, a Swedish plane manufacturer, launched its first car in 1949.

Samsung The South Korean electronics firm's name means "three stars" in Korean.

Seat Sociedad Española de Automoviles de Turismo was officially founded in 1950 in Barcelona.

Sony The Japanese electronic firm's name is taken both from a Latin word, *sonus*, which is the root of the word sonic, and from the expression "sonny boy", popular in post-war Japan when the firm was founded. The words were meant to show that the firm was a group of young people with energy and passion.

Starbucks Named after Starbuck, the mate of the *Pequod* in Herman Melville's whaling novel *Moby Dick*.

Subaru The Japanese car company takes its name from the Japanese for the star constellation called the *pleiades* or "Seven Sisters". The firm, with a logo incorporating seven stars, was formed by the merger of seven companies.

SunMicrosystems The firm's name originally stood for Stanford University Systems after the college where the founders designed their first workstation as students. They chose the name hoping to sell their product to Stanford. They failed to do so.

Tesco Sir Jack Cohen, founder of the British supermarket giant, began selling groceries in London's East End in 1919. Tesco first appeared on packets of tea in the 1920s. The name was based on the initials of T.E. Stockwell, a partner in the firm of tea suppliers, and the first two letters of Cohen.

Toyota Sakichi Toyoda first called his company Toyeda, but changed it after running a competition to find one

behind the corporate name *continued*

that sounded better. The new name is written with eight strokes in Japanese script, an auspicious number.

Vauxhall Vauxhall Iron Works was built on the site of "Fulk's Hall", the house of a medieval knight, Fulk le Breant, on the south bank of the Thames in London in 1894. *Vokzal* is the Russian word for a train station, a corruption of the name Vauxhall. Tsar Nicholas I visited the station while touring Britain and was clearly impressed. Vauxhall cars are now part of General Motors.

Volvo From the Latin meaning "I roll". It was originally a name for a ball bearing developed by the parent company of the Swedish carmaker founded in 1927.

Xerox Chestor Carlson invented a revolutionary dry-copying process as an improvement on current wet-copying methods. *Xeros* is the Greek word for dry.

Yahoo! The name is an acronym for "yet another hierarchical officious oracle", but the company's founders also liked the definition of a yahoo as "rude, unsophisticated, uncouth"

❝ yet another hierarchical officious oracle ❞

taken from the unpleasant and savage creatures in Jonathan Swift's *Gulliver's Travels*.

America's **BIGGEST** bankruptcies

Since 1980	Assets, $bn	Date
WorldCom	103.9	2002
Enron	63.4	2001
Conseco	61.4	2002
Texaco	35.9	1987
Financial Corporation of America	33.9	1988
Refco	33.3	2005
Global Crossing	30.2	2002
Pacific Gas and Electric	29.8	2001
UAL	25.2	2002
Delta Air Lines	21.8	2005
Adelphia Communications	21.5	2002
MCorp	20.2	1989
Mirant	19.4	2003
Delphi	16.6	2005
First Executive	15.2	1991
Gibraltar Financial	15.0	1990
Kmart	14.6	2002
Finova Group	14.1	2001
HomeFed	13.9	1992
Southeast Banking	13.4	1991
Reliance Group	12.6	2001
Imperial Corporation of America	12.3	1990
Federal-Mogul	10.2	2001
First City Bancorp. of Texas	9.9	1992
First Capital Holdings	9.7	1991
Baldwin-United	9.4	1983

Source: BankruptcyData.com

$elling off state assets

Privatisations: value of transactions*, $bn

	1985–1990	1991–1999	2000–2005	1985–2005
Austria	1.1	9.0	7.3	17.4
Belgium	0.1	5.6	2.4	8.1
Czech Republic	–	5.9	12.4	18.3
Denmark	–	6.6	0.5	7.1
Finland	0.4	11.0	10.2	21.5
France	5.1	52.2	67.1	124.4
Germany	3.2	48.3	45.6	97.1
Greece	–	8.2	8.8	17.0
Hungary	0.2	7.6	4.3	12.1
Ireland	–	5.9	0.8	6.7
Italy	3.3	86.0	63.3	152.6
Netherlands	1.8	10.6	16.2	28.6
Poland	0.1	11.7	13.3	25.1
Portugal	1.6	20.9	5.5	28.0
Slovakia	–	0.8	7.4	8.2
Spain	2.8	42.0	6.7	51.5
Sweden	0.1	9.7	10.7	20.5
UK	49.0	55.1	7.7	111.8

*Public offers plus private sales.
Source: Privatisation Barometer

Business blunders

America Online and Time Warner

The merger of America Online and Time Warner in 2000 was hailed as a business masterstroke for its brilliant marriage of the old technology and new. Time Warner had an extensive back catalogue of films and music, which AOL would be able to exploit through its internet distribution. America Online used its highly priced shares to create AOL Time Warner for $180 billion but the hoped for cross-media synergies failed to materialise and the collapse of the dotcom bubble wiped out much of AOL's value. The firm's shares slumped. In 2002 the company suffered the biggest ever corporate loss of some $100 billion. A year later Time Warner dropped the AOL prefix from its name.

British Airways

At the height of "cool Britannia" in 1997, BA decided that it would chime with the trend-setting mood of the nation and announced that it would do away with the union flag that decorated the tailfins of its aircraft. At a cost of some £500,000 a time, it replaced the patriotic symbol with a series of ethnic designs that represented important destinations around the world. The change was lampooned in the press, denounced by Margaret Thatcher and proved highly unpopular with British passengers (though the airline claimed that foreign travellers liked it). Virgin Airlines, a competitor, plastered Union flags all over its aircraft to the discomfort of its embattled rival. The red, white and blue tailfin motif was later restored.

The C5

Sir Clive Sinclair, a British inventor and business man, had revolutionised the electronics business and amassed a considerable fortune with his succession of ground-breaking yet affordable devices, including watches,

business b**l**u**n**d**e**r**s** *continued*

calculators and microcomputers. His innovative knack
deserted him in the field of personal transport. The C5,
launched in 1985, a battery-powered tricycle, was an
unmitigated disaster. Constructed in a vacuum-cleaner

> **❝ it was about as
> roadworthy as a
> vacuum cleaner ❞**

factory, it seemed to offer
similar levels of
roadworthiness. It looked
ridiculous; factors such as
safety and convenience seemed
to have been barely considered and very few were sold
(though it was relatively cheap). The C5 became a byword
for business failure. Never one to be deterred, Sir Clive has
suggested that the C6 is on its way.

Dasani

A costly marketing push preceded Coca-Cola's launch of
Dasani, its bottled water brand, in Britain in 2003. Further
launches in France and Germany were stymied after press
reports suggested that the "pure" water came out of a pipe
in Sidcup, an unfashionable suburb on the outskirts of
south-east London. Worse still, the entire British supply
of some 50,000 bottles had to be taken off the shelves
after a contamination scare. Despite a sophisticated
purification process, the water contained high levels of
bromate, a chemical linked with cancer. Despite these
travails in Europe, Dasani remains one of America's most
popular bottled waters.

Decca Records ... and another music
misjudgment

Dick Rowe of Decca Records turned down the chance to
sign the Beatles in 1962 saying "groups with guitars are
on their way out", though the next year he made amends
by signing the Rolling Stones. Sam Phillips, owner of a
small recording company in Memphis, Tennessee, sold

his exclusive contract with Elvis Presley to RCA Records in 1955, for $35,000. He missed out on royalties on the sale of more than 1 billion records.

Ford Edsel

The launch of the Ford Edsel in September 1957 was preceded by a big and expensive marketing campaign. Motorists eagerly awaited the arrival of Ford's mysterious new car after months of teasing advertisements announcing that "The Edsel is Coming" but without revealing what the new car looked like. The advertising effort had raised expectation to such a level that the potential buyers who flocked to showrooms in the first few days after the car went on sale were disappointed. They found a fairly ordinary vehicle with unappealing bold styling. Furthermore the extra gadgets included did not justify the high price Ford was charging compared with competing models. The Detroit giant hoped to sell some 200,000 Edsels annually but 1958 was a poor one for car sales in general. The firm sold just 64,000 in the first year. Poor quality control didn't help. Ford stopped production during the construction of the 1960 model of a vehicle which led to the mnemonic "Every Day Something Else Leaks". The firm lost $250m (equivalent to over $2 billion today) but the damage was not as severe as sometimes assumed. Ford made a profit and paid a dividend for all the time that the Edsel was produced.

> **Every Day Something Else Leaks**

Fat-finger syndrome

Fat-finger syndrome is a terrible affliction that affects those working in financial markets. In 2005, the problem, whereby hapless traders input incorrect information, hit Mizuho Securities. A cack-handed employee mistakenly typed a sell order for 610,000 shares at 1 yen in a firm called J-Com rather than one share for 610,000 yen. The Japanese financial group managed to buy back many of

business blunders *continued*

the shares and overall the error is estimated to have cost
the firm over 40 billion yen. In 2002 a trader at Eurex in
London wanted to sell one futures contract when the
DAX, Germany's leading share index, hit 5,180.
Unfortunately, he sold 5,180 contracts and the market
plummeted. The exchange later cancelled the errant
trades. In the same year, a trader at Bear Stearns, an
American investment bank, entered a $4 billion sell order
instead of one for $4m. He was blamed for a subsequent
100-point drop in the Dow Jones. In 2001 a trader at UBS
Warburg lost the Swiss investment bank £71m in a matter
of seconds while trying to sell 16 shares in Dentsu at
600,000 yen each. Instead he sold 600,000 shares in the
Japanese advertising giant at 16 yen each. The bank
managed to cancel most of the transactions. In 2001
Lehman Brothers was fined £20,000 after a trader,
wishing only to sell shares worth £3m in various blue-
chip companies, typed in too many noughts. He sold
shares worth £300m and sent the markets into freefall,
wiping 120 points and £30 billion off the FTSE 100.

Hoover

The consumer electronics firm came up with a scheme to
shift a surplus of vacuum cleaners and washing machines
in Britain. In 1992, it offered two free return flights to
Europe if customers spent just £100 on any Hoover
product. Restrictive rules and the sale of extras was
intended to cover the costs of the
promotion. While their travel
agents failed to cope with the
overwhelming response, Hoover
extended the promotion with
flights to America. "Two return seats: Unbelievable" ran
the ad's tagline. How true. Hoover was inundated by
disgruntled customers, questions were asked in
Parliament and a pressure group was formed. Customers

> **two return seats: unbelievable ran the tagline. How true**

started taking Hoover to court. The cases continued for six years. Some 220,000 people did eventually fly at a cost to Hoover of £48m and huge damage to its reputation.

The Hunt brothers' silver spree

Bunker Hunt was one of the world's richest men through the family's Texas-based oil business but he wanted more. In the early 1970s, he and his younger brother, Herbert, made some cash when, after buying 200,000 ounces of silver, prices doubled to $3 an ounce. Over the rest of the decade they purchased 59m ounces, roughly a third of the world's supply, pushing the price to $50 an ounce and earning a paper profit of about $4 billion. But the high prices led to greater supplies of scrap silver and mining investment. In 1980 silver prices fell by 80% in a matter of days. The Hunt brothers declared bankruptcy and in 1988 were convicted of conspiring to manipulate the market.

Louisiana Territory

In 1803, the United States purchased from France the Louisiana Territory, more than 2m sq km of land extending from the Mississippi River to the Rocky Mountains. The price was 60m francs, about $15m. France acquired Louisiana after Napoleon swapped it with Spain for Tuscany (which Spain never got hold of).

Manhattan Island

In 1626 the Lenape Indians sold Manhattan Island to Peter Minuit, director-general of New Netherlands Colony, a Dutch settlement, for goods valued at 60 Dutch guilders, or $24. The goods are commonly identified as trinkets and beads, though this may be a later addition to the story. Minuit was also involved in the purchase of Staten Island in return for kettles, cloth, wampum and tools. These Indian chiefs did at least do better than thousands of others who got nothing for land later appropriated in America.

business blunders *continued*

New Coke

In the early 1980s Coca-Cola executives decided that the way to fight the growing popularity of the Pepsi brand was a new formula for their soft drink. New Coke was first tested in 1985, and the company concluded that it was on to a winner. The public thought otherwise. Coke received thousands of complaints as soon as the drink was launched. These were dismissed as "relatively insignificant" at first. After three months and complaints from half a million irate customers the old Coke, renamed "Coke Classic", was back on the shelves. Conspiracy theorists argue that it was a ruse to rekindle interest in Coke. The company claimed that it wasn't clever enough to come up with an idea like that.

> **the company claimed it wasn't clever enough to come up with an idea like that**

Perrier

In 1990 American regulators said that bottles of Perrier were contaminated with traces of benzene, a chemical linked with cancer. The French producers of the sparkling mineral water claimed it was an isolated incident caused by the mistaken use of cleaning fluids at an American bottling plant and recalled 70m bottles in America and Canada. However, Dutch and Danish authorities also found traces of the chemical in Perrier, leading to a worldwide recall. The water firm then claimed that benzene occurred naturally in carbon dioxide and later blamed employees for not changing filters at its source in France. After the scandal Perrier's worldwide sales fell by nearly half and in 1992 Nestlé, a Swiss multinational, acquired the struggling firm.

Persil Power

Unilever launched Persil Power in Britain as a washing powder containing a manganese "accelerator" that removed dirt at lower temperatures. Procter & Gamble, the Anglo-Dutch firm's biggest rival, conducted research that showed that far from cleaning favourite garments, the new powder rotted clothing away. A war of words ensued in the press and through advertising but eventually Unilever was forced to withdraw Persil Power.

Ratners

Gerald Ratner, speaking at the Institute of Directors in 1991, explained why he could sell products so cheaply in his chain of high-street jewellers. He said he "sold a pair of earrings for under a pound, which is cheaper than a prawn sandwich from Marks & Spencer, but probably wouldn't last as long". He followed up by revealing that a decanter was so cheap because it

the decanter was so cheap because it was *total crap*

was "total crap". Reports in the media led to the company's shares losing £500m in value. Ratner resigned in 1992 and in 1993 the company was renamed Signet, since when it has reclaimed its position as one of the world's biggest jewellery firms. Gerald Ratner went on to set up an online jewellery business and he has expressed interest in buying the UK arm of Signet.

South African gold

In 1886 Sors Hariezon, a gold prospector from Witwatersrand in the Transvaal, sold his South African gold claim for $20. Over the next 100 years, mines sunk on or near his claim produced over 1,000 tonnes of gold a year, 70% of the supply of the precious metal in the West.

business b^luⁿd^er^s *continued*

Topman

Topman's brand chief David Shepherd said in an interview with a trade magazine that the British clothes firm's target customers were "hooligans or whatever". He carried on "Very few of our customers have to wear suits to work … They'll be for his first interview or first court case." Retail giant Arcadia, which owned Topman, said the remarks were taken out of context.

Xerox

In 1977 the office equipment firm showed its top managers an electronic typewriter that could display written correspondence on a screen, store it with a click of a button, send it around the office and print out copies. The project had taken ten years to develop but the managers were unconvinced that it had a commercial future. Meanwhile, Apple Computer emulated much of the technology and developed

managers were not convinced that it had a commercial future

the personal computer. Some 35 years earlier, IBM, Kodak and General Electric had all eschewed a new technology for rapidly reproducing copies on paper.

The Bible

Adam gave up the rights to the Garden of Eden for an apple. Esau sold his birthright for a mess of potage, though the extent of his father's estate is unknown.

BIG buck$$$$$

Profits and losses

Biggest annual profits, world ExxonMobil's $36.1 billion in 2005.

Biggest annual profits, UK Royal Dutch Shell's $25.3 billion in 2005.

Biggest annual loss, world AOL Time Warner's $98.7 billion in 2002, after massive write-downs ($45 billion and $54 billion) on the value of America Online. Vice-chairman Ted Turner resigned. The $54.2 billion loss in the fourth quarter of 2002 was also a record.

Biggest annual loss, Europe Vodafone made a net loss of £21.9 billion in the year to March 2006 after big write-offs of assets, particularly in Germany.

In Japan Mizuho Financial Group, once the world's biggest bank by assets, made a loss of ¥2.4 trillion ($19.5 billion) in the year beginning April 2002.

Market capitalisation

The highest market capitalisation of any company was Microsoft on December 27 1999 at $615 billion. Other big caps on that day, in June 2006 and at their peaks (up to June 2006) were:

$bn	Dec 27 1999	June 2006	Peak	Peak date
Microsoft	615	238	615	27/12/99
General Electric	523	343	594	20/8/00
Cisco Systems	360	119	548	27/3/00
Intel	284	111	482	22/3/00
Exxon Mobil	281	372	410	21/9/05
Wal-Mart	309	201	284	15/3/02

Sources: Company websites; press reports; Thomson Datastream

The world's mo$t valuable brand$

Most valuable brands by region, $bn

United States

Microsoft	62.0
GE (General Electric)	55.8
Coca-Cola	41.4
Marlboro	38.5
Wal-Mart	37.6
Google	37.4
IBM	36.1
Citi	31.0
McDonald's	29.0
Bank of America	28.2

Europe (Ex. UK)

Nokia	26.5
BMW	23.8
TIM (Telecom Italia Mobile)	19.6
Louis Vuitton	19.5
Mercedes	17.8
Telefónica Móviles	15.2
Deutsche Bank	13.0
Banco Santander	12.5
Porsche	12.0
T-Mobile	11.9

Asia

China Mobile	39.2
Toyota	30.2
NTT DoCoMo	19.5
Honda	14.4
Samsung	12.0
Nissan	10.9
Canon	9.9
Sony	9.4
Lexus	5.1
Mizuho Bank	4.7

UK

Vodafone	24.1
Tesco	15.5
HSBC	13.9
Orange	9.4
BP	5.5
Barclays	5.1
Asda	4.7
Lloyds TSB	4.1
O2	3.9
Marks & Spencer	3.3

Most valuable brands by sector, $bn

Apparel

Nike	Nike	10.8
H&M	H&M (Hennes & Mauritz)	8.0
Zara	Industria de Diseño Textil	5.1
Esprit	Esprit Holdings	4.2
Next	Next	3.1
Gap	Gap	2.8
Adidas	Adidas-Salomon	2.3
Ralph Lauren	Polo Ralph Lauren	1.9
Old Navy	Gap	1.8
PUMA	PUMA Rudolf Dassler Sport	1.8
Levi's	Levi Strauss	1.7
Banana Republic	Gap	1.3
Abercrombie & Fitch	Abercrombie & Fitch	1.2
American Eagle Outfitters	American Eagle Outfitters	1.1
Timberland	The Timberland Company	1.0

Automobiles

Toyota	Toyota Motor	30.2
BMW	BMW	23.8
Mercedes	DaimlerChrysler	17.8
Honda	Honda Motor	14.4
Ford	Ford Motor	13.8
Chevrolet	General Motors	12.5
Porsche	Porsche	12.0
Nissan	Nissan Motor	10.9
VW (Volkswagen)	Volkswagen	6.8
Renault	Renault	5.2
Lexus	Toyota Motor	5.1
Dodge	DaimlerChrysler	4.1
Volvo	Ford Motor	3.4
Audi	Volkswagen	3.2
Chrysler	DaimlerChrysler	3.2
Opel	General Motors	3.1
Cadillac	General Motors	2.2
GMC	General Motors	2.1
Mini	BMW	2.0
Pontiac	General Motors	1.9

the world's mo$t valuable brand$ *continued*

Beer

Budweiser	Anheuser Busch	6.8
Bud Light	Anheuser Busch	5.0
Heineken	Heineken N.V.	3.4
Guinness	Diageo	2.9
Corona	Grupo Modelo	2.6
Stella Artois	InBev	2.2
Miller Lite	SAB Miller	2.0
Skol	InBev	1.1
Amstel	Heineken N.V.	1.0

Financial institutions

Citi	Citigroup	31.0
Bank of America	Bank of America	28.2
American Express	American Express	18.8
HSBC	HSBC Holdings	13.9
Deutsche Bank	Deutsche Bank	13.0
Banco Santander	Banco Santander Central Hispano	12.5
Morgan Stanley	Morgan Stanley	10.6
Wachovia	Wachovia Corporation	10.2
Merrill Lynch	Merrill Lynch	10.1
Chase	JPMorgan Chase	9.7
UBS	UBS	9.5
Goldman Sachs	The Goldman Sachs Group	8.9
State Farm	State Farm Mutual Automobile Ins.	7.9
JPMorgan	JPMorgan Chase	7.1

Luxury goods

Louis Vuitton	LVMH	19.5
Chanel	Chanel	6.5
Cartier	Compagnie Financière Richemont	5.5
Rolex	Montres Rolex	4.9
Hermes	Hermès International	4.8
Gucci	Gucci Group	4.4
Hennessy	LVMH	4.2
Moet & Chandon	LVMH	3.7
Fendi	LVMH	3.5

Mobile communications

China Mobile	China Mobile (HK)	39.2
Vodafone	Vodafone Group	24.1
TIM	Telecom Italia Mobile	19.6
NTT DoCoMo	NTT DoCoMo	19.5
Telefónica Móviles	Telefónica	15.2
Verizon Wireless	Verizon Communications	14.9
T-Mobile	Deutsche Telekom	11.9
Orange	Orange	9.4
Cingular Wireless	Cingular Wireless	6.7
O2	O2	3.9

Technology

Microsoft	Microsoft Corporation	62.0
Google	Google	37.4
IBM	IBM	36.1
Nokia	Nokia	26.5
Intel	Intel	25.2
Cisco	Cisco Systems	20.9
HP	Hewlett-Packard	19.7
Dell	Dell	18.3
Apple	Apple Computer	16.0
Yahoo!	Yahoo!	14.1
Oracle	Oracle	13.9
Samsung	Samsung Electronics	12.0
Canon	Canon	9.9
Accenture	Accenture	9.8
SAP	SAP	9.6
Sony	Sony	9.4
Motorola	Motorola	9.1
Siemens	Siemens	6.7
Electronic Arts	Electronic Arts	5.3
Adobe	Adobe Systems	3.9
Texas Instruments	Texas Instruments	3.6
Xerox	Xerox	3.5
Philips	Royal Philips Electronics	2.7

Note: ranking is based on present-day value of the future earnings the brand is expected to generate for its current owner. Other firms arrive at different valuations; for example, Interbrand put the 2005 economic worth of Coca-Cola at $67.5bn and of Microsoft at $59.9bn.

Sources: Millward Brown Optimor; *Financial Times*

The world's most admired companies

2005	Industry	Country	Score (out of 10)
Procter & Gamble	Household and personal products	US	8.52
Walgreen	Food & drug stores	US	8.42
United Parcel Service	Delivery	US	8.38
Walt Disney	Entertainment	US	8.38
General Electric	Electronics	US	8.29
Exxon Mobil	Petroleum refining	US	8.24
Nestlé	Consumer food products	Switzerland	8.07
Anheuser-Busch	Beverages	US	8.00
Texas Instruments	Semiconductors	US	7.95
Berkshire Hathaway	Insurance: property, casualty	US	7.90
Illinois Tool Works	Industrial & farm equipment	US	7.83
Home Depot	Specialty retailers	US	7.72
IBM	Computers	US	7.67
Johnson & Johnson	Pharmaceuticals	US	7.64
DuPont	Chemicals	US	7.63
Bank of America	Mega-banks	US	7.59
Alcoa	Metals	US	7.53
Toyota Motor	Motor vehicles	Japan	7.51
Northwestern Mutual	Insurance: life, health	US	7.49
Nokia	Network communications	Finland	7.46
Cardinal Health	Wholesalers: health care	US	7.42
International Paper	Forest & paper products	US	7.31
Toyota Industries	Motor vehicle parts	Japan	7.28
Continental Airlines	Airlines	US	7.27
Areva	Energy	France	7.19
United Technologies	Aerospace and defence	US	7.18
AT&T Inc	Telecommunications	US	6.96
Takenaka	Engineering, construction	Japan	6.73

Source: *Fortune*

Britain's most admired companies ✓

2005	Industry	Score, out of 90
Tesco	Supermarkets	71.88
BP	Oil	71.04
Cadbury Schweppes	Food and drink	70.74
Unilever	Consumer products	68.54
BSkyB	Media	66.79
Serco Group	Outsourcing services	66.14
Diageo	Spirits	66.14
Vodafone	Telecommunications	66.04
Mitchells & Butlers	Food and drink	65.44
HBOS	Banking	65.07
Johnson Matthey	Catalysts	65.00
Carnival	Shipping	64.65
Man Group	Hedge-fund manager	64.40
BG Group	Natural gas	64.22
Burberry Group	Retailing	64.17
IMI	Engineering	64.11
BHP Billiton	Mining	64.00
Wolseley	Heating/plumbing equipment	63.33
Royal Bank of Scotland	Banking	63.31
Balfour Beatty	Construction	63.29
Rotork	Valves and gearboxes	63.17
Capita Group	Support services	63.09
Tomkins	Engineering	63.00
Punch Taverns	Food and drink	62.78
HSBC	Banking	62.74
Kidde	Fire-prevention equipment	62.44
Halma	Life-protection equipment	62.39
SAB Miller	Brewing	62.33
Greene King	Brewing	62.06
Rio Tinto	Mining	61.80

Note: The 10 largest public companies within 22 sectors rank their 9 sector rivals on a scale of 0-10 for 9 performance criteria including quality of management, marketing, and products & services; financials; innovation; attracting, developing and retaining talent; use of corporate assets; community & environmental responsibility; and value as a long-term investment.
Source: *Management Today*

What companies say about themselves

Anheuser Busch Our vision: Through all of our products, services and relationships, we will add to life's enjoyment.

Carlsberg Mission: Carlsberg is a dynamic, international provider of beer and beverage brands, bringing people together and adding to the enjoyment of life.

Coca-Cola The Coca-Cola Company exists to benefit and refresh everyone it touches.

Ericsson Our vision: To be the prime driver in an all-communicating world.

Ford Our Vision: to become the world's leading company for automotive products and services.

> ❝ we do the right thing for our people, our environment and our society ❞

Our Mission: we are a global, diverse family with a proud heritage, passionately committed to providing outstanding products and services.

Our Values: we do the right thing for our people, our environment and our society, but above all for our customers.

Gillette The Gillette Company's vision is to build total brand value by innovating to deliver consumer value and customer leadership faster, better and more completely than our competition.

Goldman Sachs Our culture is very much in evidence helping us attract and retain the best employees and clients. Goldman Sachs' commitment to its clients, teamwork, integrity, professional excellence and entrepreneurial spirit has its beginnings in 1869 with Marcus Goldman. This spirit is embodied today in our core values of client focus, integrity, meritocracy, excellence, entrepreneurial spirit and teamwork.

Google Google's mission is to organise the world's information and make it universally accessible and useful.
Our philosophy: Never settle for the best.
Ten things Google has found to be true

1. Focus on the user and all else will follow
2. It's best to do one thing really, really well
3. Fast is better than slow
4. Democracy on the web works
5. You don't need to be at your desk to need an answer
6. You can make money without doing evil
7. There is always more information out there
8. The need for information crosses all borders
9. You can be serious without a suit
10. Great just isn't good enough.

Heinz Our vision, quite simply, is to be "the world's premier food company, offering nutritious, superior tasting foods to people everywhere".

Johnson & Johnson We believe our first responsibility is to the doctors, nurses and patients, to mothers and fathers and all others who use our products and services.

Lagardère Where there's a will, we pave the way.

Levi Strauss & Co Our values are fundamental to our success. They are the foundation of our company, define who we are and set us apart from the competition. They underlie our vision of the future, our business strategies and our decisions, actions and behaviours. We live by them. They endure.

❝ people love our clothes and trust our company ❞

Four core values are at the heart of Levi Strauss & Co: Empathy, Originality, Integrity and Courage ...

Generations of people have worn our products as a symbol of freedom and self-expression in the face of adversity, challenge and social change. They forged a new territory called the American West. They fought in

what companies say *continued*

wars for peace. They instigated counterculture revolutions. They tore down the Berlin Wall. Reverent, irreverent – they all took a stand …

People love our clothes and trust our company. We will market the most appealing and widely worn apparel brands …

We will clothe the world.

Microsoft At Microsoft, we work to help people and businesses throughout the world realise their potential. This is our mission. Everything we do reflects this mission and the values that make it possible.

Nokia Connecting is about helping people to feel close to what matters. Wherever, whenever, Nokia believes in communicating, sharing, and in the awesome potential in connecting the 2 billion who do with the 4 billion who don't.

Pfizer Our mission: We will become the world's most valued company to patients, customers, colleagues, investors, business partners, and the communities where we work and live.

Philip Morris International Our goal is to be the most responsible, effective and respected developer, manufacturer and marketer of consumer products, especially products intended for adults. Our core business is manufacturing and marketing the best quality tobacco products to adults who use them.

Procter & Gamble We will provide branded products and services of superior quality and value that improve the lives of the world's consumers. As a result, consumers will reward us with leadership sales, profit, and value creation, allowing our people, our shareholders, and the communities in which we live and work to prosper.

Royal Mail Through our trusted brands, we reach everbody every working day in mail, parcels and express services and Post Office branches. Today, we are reinventing our business to meet the changing needs of our customers and the demands of competition. Our goal is to be the world's leading postal service.

Tesco Our core purpose is to create value for customers to earn their lifetime loyalty.

Our success depends on people. The people who shop with us and the people who work with us. If our customers like what we offer, they are more likely to come back and shop with us again. If the Tesco team find what we do rewarding, they are more likely to go that extra mile to help our customers.

This is expressed as two key values:

- No one tries harder for customers, and
- Treat people as we like to be treated.

Unilever Mission: To add vitality to life. We meet everyday needs for nutrition, hygiene, and personal care with brands that help people feel good, look good and get more out of life.

Virgin We believe in making a difference. In our customers' eyes, Virgin stands for value for money, quality, innovation, fun and a sense of competitive challenge.

Source: Company websites

Games directors play

Although routinely presented as a serious, analytical and rational process, boardroom behaviour is often intensely political, involving personal rivalries and power plays. The games directors play include the following.

- **Alliance building** is played outside the boardroom for ensuring mutual support within. It is closely allied to log rolling.

- **Coalition building** involves canvassing support for an issue informally outside the boardroom so that there is a sufficient consensus when the matter is discussed formally.

- **Cronyism** is supporting a director's interests even though they may not be in the best interest of the company or its shareholders. For example, a director declares a personal interest in a contract in a tender being discussed by the board; he might even leave the room for the discussion. However, board members support his bid because of their relationship, even though it is not the most worthy. This is sometimes alleged to be the basis of corporate governance in Asia.

> **Cronyism… is sometimes alleged to be the basis of corporate governance in Asia**

- **Deal making** is a classic game usually involving compromise, in which two or more directors reach a behind-the-scenes agreement to achieve a specific outcome in a board decision.

- **Divide and rule** is a dirty game, in which the player sees the chance to set one director against another, or groups of directors against each other. An issue in the financial accounts might be used, for example, to set the executive directors, the non-executive directors and the auditors against each other in order to achieve an entirely different personal aim.

- **Empire building** is the misuse of privileged access to information, people or other resources to acquire power over organisational territory. The process often involves intrigue, battles and conquests.

- **Half truths** occur if a director, although not deliberately lying, tells only one side of the issue in board deliberations.

- **Hidden agendas** involve directors' pursuit of secret goals to benefit their own empire or further their own career against the interest of the organisation as a whole.

- **Log rolling** occurs when director A agrees, off the record, to support director B's interests, for mutual support when it comes to matters of interest to A.

- **Propaganda** is the dissemination of information to support a cause and is seen more in relationships with shareholders, stockmarkets and financial institutions than in board-level deliberations. The regulatory authorities are likely to act if propaganda becomes excessive or deliberately false.

- **Rival camps** is a game played when there are opposing factions on a board, in which hostilities, spies and double agents can be involved.

- **Scaremongering** emphasises the downside risks in a board decision, casting doubts about a situation, so that a proposal will be turned down.

- **Snowing** involves executive directors deluging an outside director seeking further information with masses of data confusing the situation and papering over any cracks.

- **Spinning** is an art form developed at governmental level, which presents a distorted view of a person or a situation, favourable to the interests of the spinner. In corporate governance,

> **Spinning... is an art form developed at governmental level**

games directors play *continued*

spinning can be carried out at the level of the board, the shareholders or the media.

- **Sponsorship** is support by a powerful director for another, usually for their joint benefit.

- **Suboptimisation** occurs when a director supports a part of the organisation to the detriment of the company as a whole. Some executive directors suffer from tunnel vision because they are too closely involved with a functional department or a subsidiary company, and from short-sighted myopia because they will be personally affected by the outcome.

> **Some executive directors suffer from tunnel vision**

- **Window dressing** produces a fine external show of sound corporate governance principles while covering up failures. Window dressing can also involve showing financial results in the best possible light while hiding weaknesses.

Source: *Essential Director*, R.I. (Bob) Tricker, The Economist/Profile Books

Business *friendliness*

Business environment index

2006–10, score out of 10

Denmark	8.77	Portugal	7.35	Russia	6.06
Finland	8.72	Hungary	7.34	Serbia and	
Singapore	8.69	Slovenia	7.28	Montenegro	6.01
Canada	8.69	Qatar	7.27	Peru	5.91
US	8.68	Bahrain	7.16	Egypt	5.91
Netherlands	8.64	Latvia	7.15	Sri Lanka	5.81
UK	8.63	Lithuania	7.15	Jordan	5.78
Switzerland	8.60	Poland	7.14	Kazakhstan	5.67
Hong Kong	8.60	Italy	7.08	Vietnam	5.65
Ireland	8.57	Cyprus	6.95	Dominican	
Sweden	8.46	Thailand	6.89	Republic	5.51
Australia	8.41	Mexico	6.88	Ukraine	5.43
New Zealand	8.37	South Africa	6.86	Morocco	5.34
Germany	8.36	Greece	6.80	Tunisia	5.31
Belgium	8.28	Brazil	6.78	Azerbaijan	5.27
Norway	8.21	Bulgaria	6.68	Pakistan	5.23
Austria	8.17	Kuwait	6.62	Algeria	5.20
France	8.07	Romania	6.58	Ecuador	5.19
Taiwan	8.05	Croatia	6.47	Nigeria	4.83
Spain	7.90	Saudi Arabia	6.42	Venezuela	4.77
Estonia	7.84	Costa Rica	6.41	Kenya	4.72
Chile	7.83	China	6.36	Bangladesh	4.65
Israel	7.78	Colombia	6.33	Iran	4.43
Czech Republic	7.52	Turkey	6.32	Libya	4.38
Slovakia	7.50	Philippines	6.30	Cuba	3.96
South Korea	7.46	Argentina	6.24	Angola	3.61
Japan	7.45	El Salvador	6.24	*Median*	*6.87*
Malaysia	7.41	Indonesia	6.20	*Average*	*6.79*
UAE	7.35	India	6.13		

Note. Based on macroeconomic and political environment, foreign investment policy, tax regime, labour market, and infrastructure.

Source: Economist Intelligence Unit

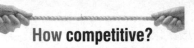

How competitive?

Growth competitiveness index, 2005

Finland	5.94	Slovenia	4.59
US	5.81	Kuwait	4.58
Sweden	5.65	Cyprus	4.54
Denmark	5.65	Malta	4.54
Taiwan	5.58	Thailand	4.50
Singapore	5.48	Bahrain	4.48
Iceland	5.48	Czech Republic	4.42
Switzerland	5.46	Hungary	4.38
Norway	5.40	Tunisia	4.32
Australia	5.21	Slovakia	4.31
Netherlands	5.21	South Africa	4.31
Japan	5.18	Lithuania	4.30
UK	5.11	Latvia	4.29
Canada	5.10	Jordan	4.28
Germany	5.10	Greece	4.26
New Zealand	5.09	Italy	4.21
South Korea	5.07	Botswana	4.21
UAE	4.99	China	4.07
Qatar	4.97	India	4.04
Estonia	4.95	Poland	4.00
Austria	4.95	Mauritius	4.00
Portugal	4.91	Egypt	3.96
Chile	4.91	Uruguay	3.93
Malaysia	4.90	Mexico	3.92
Luxembourg	4.90	El Salvador	3.86
Ireland	4.86	Colombia	3.84
Israel	4.84	Bulgaria	3.83
Hong Kong	4.83	Ghana	3.82
Spain	4.80	Trinidad and Tobago	3.81
France	4.78	Kazakhstan	3.77
Belgium	4.63	Croatia	3.74

Note: Based on macroeconomic environment, quality of public institutions, and level of technological readiness and innovation. A higher score indicates greater competitiveness.
Source: World Economic Forum

Easy money?

Accessibility of capital to entrepreneurs, max = 10, 2005

UK	8.01	Saudi Arabia	5.56
Hong Kong	7.84	Kuwait	5.52
Singapore	7.77	Lithuania	5.51
US	7.75	Hungary	5.36
Sweden	7.62	Oman	5.30
Denmark	7.61	China	5.17
Australia	7.60	UAE	5.14
Norway	7.47	Brazil	5.13
Finland	7.46	Panama	5.13
Canada	7.42	Jordan	5.11
Ireland	7.42	Mexico	5.05
Switzerland	7.39	Slovakia	5.05
Netherlands	7.20	Poland	4.98
New Zealand	7.04	Latvia	4.92
Germany	6.93	El Salvador	4.90
Malaysia	6.88	Lebanon	4.87
Spain	6.80	Peru	4.69
Chile	6.78	Colombia	4.68
Japan	6.76	Russia	4.67
France	6.62	Tunisia	4.67
Estonia	6.59	Bulgaria	4.58
Austria	6.41	India	4.58
South Korea	6.37	Slovenia	4.56
South Africa	6.36	Costa Rica	4.49
Taiwan	6.34	Indonesia	4.48
Portugal	6.31	Philippines	4.44
Israel	6.19	Morocco	4.40
Belgium	6.17	Turkey	4.37
Greece	5.85	Namibia	4.34
Thailand	5.71	Papua New Guinea	4.31
Italy	5.66	Croatia	4.30
Czech Republic	5.58	Sri Lanka	4.27

Note: Based on over 50 measures such as strength of banking system and the diversity of financial markets.
Source: Milken Institute

Business cycles

America's ten-year expansion from March 1991 to March 2001 was the longest in the 150 years covered by the National Bureau of Economic Research's data.

America's business cycle dates, duration in months

Peak	Trough	Peak to trough	Trough to peak	Trough to trough	Peak to peak
Feb-45	Oct-45	8	80	88	93
Nov-48	Oct-49	11	37	48	45
Jul-53	May-54	10	45	55	56
Aug-57	Apr-58	8	39	47	49
Apr-60	Feb-61	10	24	34	32
Dec-69	Nov-70	11	106	117	116
Nov-73	Mar-75	16	36	52	47
Jan-80	Jul-80	6	58	64	74
Jul-81	Nov-82	16	12	28	18
Jul-90	Mar-91	8	92	100	108
Mar-01	Nov-01	8	120	128	128

Source: National Bureau of Economic Research

The Economic Cycle Research Institute in New York covers data for 20 countries from 1948. It shows that:

The UK rose from a trough in August 1952 to a peak in September 1974, fell briefly to a trough 11 months later, then there was a peak in June 1979, a trough in May 1981, a long expansion to a peak in May 1990 and a short fall to a trough in March 1992.

Japan had a long expansion period from December 1954 to November 1973, contracted briefly then had another long period of growth until April 1992. After several short cycles the economy reached a trough in September 2003.

Business start-ups and *failures*

US

	Start-ups, '000	Shut-downs, '000
1995	594	497
1996	598	512
1997	591	530
1998	590	541
1999	580	544
2000	574	543
2001	585	553
2002	570	587
2003	612	541

Note: Years are to end March.
Source: Office of Advocacy, US Small Business Administration

UK

	VAT registrations, '000	VAT deregistrations, '000
1995	161.5	161.2
1996	165.9	150.0
1997	182.4	144.8
1998	182.0	144.3
1999	176.6	148.5
2000	178.6	153.3
2001	169.3	151.9
2002	176.2	155.7
2003	189.1	167.6
2004	181.4	179.4

Note: Value-added tax threshold at the start of 2004 was an annual turnover of £56,000; 1.8m of the
estimated 4.3m enterprises in the UK were VAT-registered.
Source: National Statistics, Small Business Service

Corruption: business perceptions

2005, 10=least corrupt

Bangladesh	1.7	Uganda	2.5
Chad	1.7	Belarus	2.6
Haiti	1.8	Eritrea	2.6
Myanmar	1.8	Honduras	2.6
Turkmenistan	1.8	Kazakhstan	2.6
Côte d'Ivoire	1.9	Nicaragua	2.6
Equatorial Guinea	1.9	Palestine	2.6
Nigeria	1.9	Ukraine	2.6
Angola	2.0	Vietnam	2.6
Congo-Kinshasa	2.1	Zambia	2.6
Kenya	2.1	Zimbabwe	2.6
Pakistan	2.1	Gambia	2.7
Paraguay	2.1	Macedonia	2.7
Somalia	2.1	Swaziland	2.7
Sudan	2.1	Yemen	2.7
Tajikistan	2.1	Algeria	2.8
Azerbaijan	2.2	Argentina	2.8
Cameroon	2.2	Madagascar	2.8
Ethiopia	2.2	Malawi	2.8
Indonesia	2.2	Mozambique	2.8
Iraq	2.2	Serbia and Montenegro	2.8
Liberia	2.2	Armenia	2.9
Uzbekistan	2.2	Benin	2.9
Burundi	2.3	Bosnia and Herzegovina	2.9
Cambodia	2.3	Gabon	2.9
Congo-Brazzaville	2.3	India	2.9
Georgia	2.3	Iran	2.9
Kyrgyzstan	2.3	Mali	2.9
Papua New Guinea	2.3	Moldova	2.9
Venezuela	2.3	Tanzania	2.9
Albania	2.4	Dominican Republic	3.0
Niger	2.4	Mongolia	3.0
Russia	2.4	Romania	3.0
Sierra Leone	2.4	Lebanon	3.1
Afghanistan	2.5	Rwanda	3.1
Bolivia	2.5	China	3.2
Ecuador	2.5	Morocco	3.2
Guatemala	2.5	Senegal	3.2
Guyana	2.5	Sri Lanka	3.2
Libya	2.5	Suriname	3.2
Nepal	2.5	Laos	3.3
Philippines	2.5	Burkina Faso	3.4

Croatia	3.4	Jordan	5.7
Egypt	3.4	Bahrain	5.8
Lesotho	3.4	Botswana	5.9
Poland	3.4	Qatar	5.9
Saudi Arabia	3.4	Taiwan	5.9
Syria	3.4	Uruguay	5.9
Ghana	3.5	Slovenia	6.1
Mexico	3.5	UAE	6.2
Panama	3.5	Israel	6.3
Peru	3.5	Oman	6.3
Turkey	3.5	Estonia	6.4
Jamaica	3.6	Portugal	6.5
Belize	3.7	Malta	6.6
Brazil	3.7	Barbados	6.9
Cuba	3.8	Spain	7.0
Thailand	3.8	Chile	7.3
Trinidad and Tobago	3.8	Japan	7.3
Bulgaria	4.0	Belgium	7.4
Colombia	4.0	Ireland	7.4
Fiji	4.0	France	7.5
Seychelles	4.0	US	7.6
Costa Rica	4.2	Germany	8.2
El Salvador	4.2	Hong Kong	8.3
Latvia	4.2	Canada	8.4
Mauritius	4.2	Luxembourg	8.5
Czech Republic	4.3	Netherlands	8.6
Greece	4.3	UK	8.6
Namibia	4.3	Austria	8.7
Slovakia	4.3	Australia	8.8
South Africa	4.5	Norway	8.9
Kuwait	4.7	Switzerland	9.1
Lithuania	4.8	Sweden	9.2
Tunisia	4.9	Singapore	9.4
Hungary	5.0	Denmark	9.5
Italy	5.0	Finland	9.6
South Korea	5.0	New Zealand	9.6
Malaysia	5.1	Iceland	9.7
Cyprus	5.7		

Note: This index ranks countries based on how much corruption is perceived by business people, academics and risk analysts to exist among politicians and public officials.
Source: Transparency International

Business : ratios

These are ratios commonly used in corporate financial analysis.

Working capital

Working capital ratio = current assets/current liabilities, where current assets = stock + debtors + cash at bank and in hand + quoted investments, etc, current liabilities = creditors + overdraft at bank + taxation + dividends, etc. The ratio varies according to type of trade and conditions; a ratio from 1 to 3 is usual, with a ratio above 2 taken to be safe.

Liquidity ratio = liquid ("quick") assets/current liabilities, where liquid assets = debtors + cash at bank and in hand + quoted investments (that is, assets which can be realised within a month or so, which may not apply to all investments); current liabilities are those which may need to be repaid within the same short period, which may not necessarily include a bank overdraft where it is likely to be renewed. The liquidity ratio is sometimes referred to as the "acid test"; a ratio under 1 suggests a possibly difficult situation, while too high a ratio may mean that assets are not being usefully employed.

Turnover of working capital = sales/average working capital. The ratio varies according to type of trade; generally a low ratio can mean poor use of resources, while too high a ratio can mean over-trading. Average working capital or average stock is found by taking the opening and closing working capital or stock and dividing by 2.

Turnover of stock = sales/average stock, or (where cost of sales is known) cost of sales/average stock. The cost of sales turnover figure is to be preferred as both figures are then on the same valuation basis. This ratio can be expressed as number of times per year, or time taken for stock to be turned over once = (52/number of times) weeks. A low turnover of stock can be a sign of stocks that are difficult to move, and usually indicates adverse conditions.

Turnover of debtors = sales/average debtors. This indicates efficiency in collecting accounts. An average credit period of about one month is usual, but varies according to credit stringency conditions in the economy.

Turnover of creditors = purchases/average creditors. Average payment period is best maintained in line with turnover of debtors.

Sales

Export ratio = exports as a percentage of sales.

Sales per employee = sales/average number of employees.

Assets

Ratios of assets can vary according to the measure of assets used:

Total assets = current assets + fixed assets + other assets, where fixed assets = property + plant and machinery + motor vehicles, etc, and other assets = long-term investment + goodwill, etc.

Net assets ("net worth") = total assets – total liabilities = share capital + reserves

Turnover of net assets = sales/average net assets. As for turnover of working capital, a low ratio can mean poor use of resources.

Assets per employee = assets/average number of employees. This indicates the amount of investment backing for employees.

business : ratios *continued*

Profits

Profit margin = (profit/sales) × 100 = profits as a percentage of sales; usually profits before tax.

Profitability = (profit/total assets) × 100 = profits as a percentage of total assets.

Return on capital = (profit/net assets) × 100 = profits as a percentage of net assets ("net worth" or "capital employed").

Profit per employee = profit/average number of employees.

Earnings per share (eps) = after-tax profit – minorities/average number of shares in issue.

Entrepreneurial activity

% of the labour force either actively involved in starting a new business or owner or manager of a business that is less than 42 months old

	2000	2001	2002	2003	2004	2005
US	16.6	11.6	10.5	11.9	11.3	12.4
UK	6.9	7.8	5.4	6.4	6.3	6.2
France	5.6	7.4	3.2	1.6	6.0	5.4
Germany	7.5	8.0	5.2	5.2	4.5	5.4

Source: Department of Trade & Industry/Global Entrepreneurship Monitor

Busine$$ costs

2005	US=100
Germany	107.4
Japan	106.9
US	100.0
UK	98.1
Italy	97.8
Netherlands	95.7
France	95.6
Canada	94.5
Australia	91.5
Singapore	77.1

Note: Based on 17 industries within manufacturing, R&D, software and corporate services; and 27 cost components grouped under labour, facilities, transportation, utility, taxes and income.
Source: Competitive Alternatives, KPMG

Office occupancy costs
Total annual rent, taxes and operating expenses

May 2006	$ per sq. metre per year
London (West End)	2,079
Tokyo (Inner Central)	1,400
Hong Kong	1,094
Moscow	1,020
Mumbai	1,002
Paris	993
New York (Midtown)	593
Frankfurt	582
Singapore	447
Sydney	426
Beijing	407
Mexico City	392
Istanbul	333
Buenos Aires	307
Bangkok	217

Source: Richard Ellis

The changing workforce

Numbers of workers, m

	Canada	France	Germany	Italy	Japan	UK	US
1970	8.7	21.6	35.4	21.1	53.3	25.6	87.3
1980	12.2	23.2	37.5	22.8	57.2	26.9	117.2
1990	13.7	24.7	39.9	24.1	63.6	28.6	125.7
2000	15.8	26.7	39.7	23.7	67.7	29.4	140.9
2004	17.2	27.4	40.0	24.2*	66.4	29.4	147.4

Unemployment trends, % of labour force

	Canada	France	Germany	Italy	Japan	UK	US
1980	7.5	6.1	…	7.6	2.0	6.8	7.1
1982	11.0	7.8	…	8.5	2.3	10.9	9.7
1984	11.3	9.5	…	10.1	2.7	11.8	7.5
1985	10.7	10.2	…	10.3	2.6	11.3	7.2
1986	9.6	10.1	…	11.2	2.8	11.2	7.0
1987	8.8	10.6	…	12.0	2.9	10.8	6.2
1988	7.8	10.1	…	12.1	2.5	8.8	5.5
1989	7.5	9.5	…	12.1	2.2	7.2	5.3
1990	8.1	9.2	…	11.4	2.1	6.8	5.6
1991	10.3	9.0	6.6	11.0	2.1	8.4	6.8
1992	11.2	10.0	7.9	11.6	2.2	9.7	7.5
1993	11.4	11.1	9.5	10.0	2.5	10.3	6.9
1994	10.4	12.3	10.3	11.0	2.9	9.6	6.1
1995	9.4	11.6	10.1	11.4	3.2	8.6	5.6
1996	9.6	12.1	8.8	11.5	3.4	8.2	5.4
1997	9.1	12.3	9.8	11.6	3.4	7.1	4.9
1998	8.3	11.8	9.7	11.6	4.1	6.1	4.5
1999	7.6	11.7	8.8	11.3	4.7	6.0	4.2
2000	6.8	10.0	7.9	10.5	4.8	5.5	4.0
2001	7.2	8.8	7.9	9.5	5.0	4.8	4.7
2002	7.7	8.9	8.7	9.0	5.4	5.1	5.8
2003	7.6	9.7	10.0	8.7	5.3	4.8	6.0
2004	7.2	9.9	11.0	…	4.7	4.6	5.5

* 2003
Source International Labour Organisation

The sex divide

	Male, m	Female, m	Male, %	Female, %
Canada				
1985*	6.76	4.98	57.6	42.4
2004	8.48	7.47	53.2	46.8
% change			-7.6	10.4
France				
1973	13.43	7.73	63.5	36.5
2004	13.44	11.28	54.4	45.6
% change			-14.3	24.9
Germany				
1991*	21.88	15.57	58.4	41.6
2004	19.68	15.98	55.2	44.8
% change			-5.5	7.7
Italy				
1973	13.81	5.34	72.1	27.9
2003†	13.77	8.37	62.2	37.8
% change			-13.7	35.5
Japan				
1973	32.35	20.23	61.5	38.8
2004	37.13	26.16	58.7	41.3
% change			-4.6	7.3
UK				
1973	13.77	8.89	60.8	39.2
2004	15.04	12.97	53.7	46.3
% change			-11.7	18.1
US				
1973	52.35	32.72	61.5	38.5
2004	74.52	64.73	53.5	46.5
% change			-13.0	20.8

* First year available.

† Last year available.

Source: International Labour Organisation

Days lost in strikes and lockouts

Man days, m

	Canada	France	Germany	Italy	Japan	UK	US
1971	2.87	4.39	...	14.80	6.03	13.55	47.59
1972	7.75	3.76	...	19.50	5.15	23.91	27.07
1973	5.78	3.91	...	23.42	4.60	7.20	27.95
1974	9.22	3.38	...	19.47	9.66	14.75	31.81
1975	10.91	3.87	...	27.19	8.02	6.01	17.56
1976	11.61	4.05	...	25.38	3.25	3.28	23.96
1977	3.31	2.43	...	16.57	1.52	10.14	21.26
1978	7.39	2.08	...	10.18	1.36	9.41	23.77
1979	7.83	3.17	...	27.53	0.93	29.47	20.41
1980	8.98	1.52	...	16.46	1.00	11.96	20.84
1981	8.88	1.44	...	10.53	0.55	4.27	16.91
1982	5.80	2.25	...	18.56	0.54	5.31	9.06
1983	4.44	1.32	...	14.00	0.51	3.75	17.46
1984	3.88	1.32	...	8.70	0.35	27.14	8.50
1985	3.13	0.73	...	3.83	0.26	6.40	7.08
1986	7.15	0.57	...	5.64	0.25	1.92	11.86
1987	3.81	0.51	...	4.61	0.26	3.55	4.47
1988	4.90	1.09	...	3.32	0.17	3.70	4.38
1989	3.70	0.80	...	4.44	0.22	4.13	16.53
1990	5.08	0.53	...	5.18	0.14	1.90	5.93
1991	2.52	0.50	...	2.99	0.10	0.76	4.58
1992	2.11	0.36	...	2.74	0.23	0.53	3.99
1993	1.52	0.51	0.59	3.41	0.12	0.65	3.98
1994	1.61	0.50	0.23	3.37	0.09	0.28	5.02
1995	1.58	0.78	0.25	0.91	0.08	0.42	5.77
1996	3.35	0.44	0.10	1.93	0.04	1.30	4.89
1997	3.61	0.39	0.05	1.16	0.11	0.23	4.50
1998	2.44	0.35	0.02	0.58	0.10	0.28	5.12
1999	2.45	0.57	0.08	0.91	0.09	0.24	2.00
2000	1.66	0.81	0.01	0.88	0.04	0.50	20.42
2001	2.20	0.69	0.03	1.03	0.03	0.53	1.15
2002	3.03	...	0.31	4.86	0.01	1.32	0.66
2003	1.74	...	0.16	1.96	0.01	0.50	4.08
2004	3.26	...	0.05	0.69	...	0.90	1.02

Source: International Labour Organisation

Labour union strength

Latest year

	Union members, m	% of workforce
Australia	1.9	23
Belgium	2.7	58
Brazil	17.4	44
Canada	3.6	30
China	134.0	90
Colombia	1.1	29
Denmark	2.1	87
Finland	2.2	100
France	6.0	31
Germany	8.3	26
Hong Kong	0.7	21
Iceland	0.1	92
India	6.4	na
Ireland	0.5	39
Japan	10.3	19
Malaysia	0.8	na
Netherlands	1.9	27
New Zealand	0.3	18
Norway	1.5	72
Pakistan	0.3	na
Philippines	3.9	27
Singapore	0.4	24
Slovakia	0.7	39
South Africa	2.5	58
South Korea	1.6	11
Sweden	3.7	98
Switzerland	0.8	26
Taiwan	2.9	38
Turkey	2.6	58
UK	6.8	29
US	15.7	13

Source: International Labour Organisation

Changes in working hours

Average annual hours worked per employed person

	1950	2000	2005
Australia	1,838	1,855	1,811
Austria	1,976	1,632	1,636
Belgium	2,283	1,545	1,534
Canada	1,967	1,766	1,737
Denmark	2,283	1,554	1,551
Finland	2,035	1,750	1,700
France	1,926	1,592	1,535
Germany	2,316	1,468	1,435
Ireland	2,250	1,696	1,638
Italy	1,997	1,855	1,791
Japan	2,166	1,821	1,775
Netherlands	2,208	1,368	1,367
Norway	2,101	1,380	1,360
Spain	2,200	1,815	1,775
Sweden	1,951	1,625	1,587
UK	1,958	1,708	1,672
US	1,867	1,841	1,804

Source: OECD

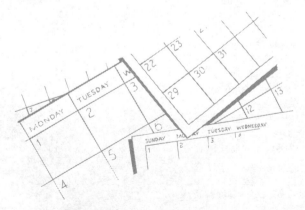

BIGGEST business employers

2005

Wal-Mart (US)	1,800,000
China National Petroleum (China)	1,090,232
State Grid (China)	844,031
U.S. Postal Service (US)	803,000
Sinopec (China)	730,800
Deutsche Post (Germany)	502,545
Agricultural Bank of China (China)	478,895
UES of Russia (Russia)	461,200
Siemens (Germany)	461,000
McDonald's (US)	447,000
Carrefour (France)	440,479
Compass Group (US)	410,074
China Telecommunications (China)	407,982
United Parcel Service (US)	407,000
Gazprom (Russia)	396,571
DaimlerChrysler (Germany/US)	382,724
Industrial & Commercial Bank of China (China)	361,623
Hitachi (Japan)	355,879
Sears Holdings (US)	355,000
Volkswagen (Germany)	344,902
Target (US)	338,000
General Motors (US)	335,000
Matsushita Electric Industrial (Japan)	334,402
China State Construction (China)	332,585
Intl. Business Machines (US)	329,373
Sodexho Alliance (France)	324,446
General Electric (US)	316,000
La Poste (France)	303,405
Citigroup (US)	303,000
China Construction Bank (US)	300,288

Source: *Fortune*

International pay comparisons ꙅnoꙅiɿɒqmoɔ

Gross salary $000, 2003	Labourer (general)	Labourer (skilled)	Professional (junior)	Professional (senior)	Management (lower middle)	Management (upper middle)
Argentina	6.1	9.5	14.9	23.2	36.9	60.4
Australia	29.1	34.3	43.3	58.5	78.9	107.3
Brazil	7.5	12.4	20.7	34.3	52.2	88.0
Canada	28.7	38.1	50.5	66.9	88.6	117.4
China	4.1	6.9	11.7	19.8	33.3	56.3
France	18.9	26.3	36.6	50.9	70.7	98.3
Germany	32.4	43.1	57.4	76.4	101.7	135.4
Hong Kong	18.1	26.7	39.6	58.6	86.7	128.4
India	3.1	5.1	8.4	14.0	23.1	38.3
Indonesia	2.7	4.6	7.9	13.4	22.7	38.6
Ireland	31.6	40.7	52.5	67.8	87.5	112.9
Italy	18.3	26.1	37.2	53.0	75.6	107.7
Japan	37.1	46.9	59.1	74.5	94.0	118.6
Mexico	8.9	14.2	22.6	36.0	65.9	105.2
Netherlands	25.6	34.8	47.3	64.4	87.7	119.3
Singapore	14.3	20.5	29.4	42.2	60.5	86.8
South Korea	23.9	30.9	40.1	52.0	67.3	87.3
Spain	25.3	33.4	44.2	58.5	77.3	102.2
Taiwan	14.8	20.8	29.3	41.1	57.8	81.2
Thailand	3.6	6.1	10.3	17.4	29.6	50.2
UK	23.7	32.8	45.3	62.7	86.8	120.1
US	26.9	32.9	39.6	52.4	69.4	93.0

Source: Mercer Human Resource Consulting

What CEOs get paid

$, 2005

	Basic compensation*	Other remuneration†
Argentina	185,649	245,651
Australia	367,952	339,795
Belgium	398,543	588,845
Brazil	295,919	553,027
Canada	401,795	667,169
Hong Kong	356,458	294,880
China‡	77,029	134,226
France	482,717	719,428
Germany	436,127	745,165
India	129,565	161,288
Italy	465,893	671,434
Japan	306,379	237,185
Malaysia	166,153	235,858
Mexico	486,312	516,046
Netherlands	368,832	493,879
Poland	235,874	160,592
Singapore	374,206	659,069
South Africa	252,194	730,730
South Korea	282,633	301,439
Spain	349,420	348,271
Sweden	394,628	554,362
Switzerland	552,890	838,009
Taiwan	167,195	83,017
UK	511,713	673,224
US	601,700	1,563,252
Venezuela	181,469	286,399

*Includes base salary and fixed bonus.
†Includes variable bonus, company contributions, perquisites and long-term incentives.
‡Shanghai.
Note: The data represent estimates of typical pay as of April 1st 2005 in industrial companies with approx $500m in annual sales.
Source: Towers Perrin

US chief executive pay

2005	Company	Total compensation $m
Richard Fairbank	Capital One Financial	249.42
Terry Semel	Yahoo!	230.56*
Henry Silverman	Cendant	139.96
Bruce Karatz	KB Home	135.53
Richard Fuld	Lehman Brothers	122.67
Ray Irani	Occidental Petroleum	80.73
Lawrence Ellison	Oracle	75.33
John Thompson	Symantec	71.84
Edwin Crawford	Caremark Rx	69.66
Angelo Mozilo	Countrywide Financial	68.96*
John Chambers	Cisco Systems	62.99
Chad Dreier	Ryland Group	56.47
Lew Frankfort	Coach	55.99
Ara Hovnanian	Hovnanian Enterprises	47.83
John Drosdick	Sunoco	46.19
Robert Toll	Toll Brothers	41.31
Robert Ulrich	Target	39.64*
Kevin Rollins	Dell	39.32*
Clarence Cazalot	Marathon Oil	37.48
David Novak	Yum Brands	37.42
Mark Papa	EOG Resources	36.54
Henri Termeer	Genzyme	36.38
Richard Adkerson	Freeport Copper	35.41
Kevin Sharer	Amgen	34.49
Jay Sugarman	iStar Financial	32.94*
George David	United Technologies	32.73
Bob Simpson	XTO Energy	32.19
Terrence Lanni	MGM Mirage	31.54
Paul Jacobs	Qualcomm	31.44
Stephen Bollenbach	Hilton Hotels	31.44*

* 2004
Source: *Forbes*

Leading Wall $treet traders' $alaries

2005, estimates		$m
Mark McGoldrick	Goldman Sachs	40-50
Raanan Agus	Goldman Sachs	30-40
Ken Karl	UBS	30-40
Boaz Weinstein	Deutsche Bank	30-40
Simon Greenshields	Morgan Stanley	20-25
Jonathan Hoffman	Lehman Brothers	20-25
Michael Hutchins	UBS	20-25
Rajeev Misra	Deutsche Bank	20-25
Arvind Raghunathan	Deutsche Bank	20-25
Olav Refvik	Morgan Stanley	20-25
John Shapiro	Morgan Stanley	20-25
Ashok Varadhan	Goldman Sachs	20-25
Barry Witlin	Merrill Lynch	20-25
Jon Wood	UBS	20-25
John Bertuzzi	Goldman Sachs	15-20
George "Beau" Taylor	JPMorgan	15-20
Driss Ben-Brahim	Goldman Sachs	10-15
Vincent Kaminski	Citigroup	10-15
Eric Rosen	JPMorgan	10-15
Christopher Ryan	UBS	10-15

Source: *Trader*

City of London total bonuses, £bn

1998	2.53	2004	6.44
1999	3.85	2005	7.49
2000	5.37	2006	8.57
2001	4.91	2007	8.83
2002	4.56	2008	9.13
2003	4.90	2009	10.43

Note: 1998–2005 are estimates, 2006-09 are forecasts.
Source: Centre for Business and Economic Research

Inve$tment banker$' pay

2005	Citigroup	Goldman Sachs	JPMorgan Chase
	Sanford I. Weill Chairman $21.5m	Henry M. Paulson Chairman & CEO $31.2m	William B. Harrison, Jr. Chairman $22.3m
	Charles Prince CEO $23.0m	Lloyd C. Blankfein President & COO $31.1m	James Dimon President & CEO $22.3m
	Robert Druskin CEO & President, corporate and investment banking $12.6m	David A. Viniar CFO $19.9m	Steven D. Black Co-Chief Executive Officer, investment bank $19.0m

2005	Lehman Brothers	Merrill Lynch	Morgan Stanley
	R.S. Fuld, Jr. Chairman & CEO $29.9m	E. Stanley O'Neal Chairman & CEO $37.0m	John J. Mack Chairman & CEO $27.0m
	J.M. Gregory President & COO $23.9m	Dow Kim Executive Vice President $28.0m	Zoe Cruz Co-President $21.1m
	D. Goldfarb Chief Administrative Officer $11.5m	Gregory J. Fleming Executive Vice President $23.0m	Neal A. Shear Co-head of institutional sales and trading $25.2m

Note: Includes annual compensation (base salary, cash bonus, other annual compensation), long-term compensation awards (restricted stock awards, securities underlying options), and all other compensation.
Source: Company reports

Best paid hedge-fund managers in the US

2005	Company	$ million
James Simons	Renaissance Technologies Corporation	1,500
T. Boone Pickens Jr.	BP Capital Management	1,400
George Soros	Soros Fund Management	840
Steven Cohen	SAC Capital Advisors	550
Paul Tudor Jones II	Tudor Investment Corporation	500
Edward Lampert	ESL Investments	425
Bruce Kovner	Caxton Associates	400
David Tepper	Appaloosa Management	400
David Shaw	D.E. Shaw & Co.	340
Stephen Mandel Jr.	Lone Pine Capital	275
Israel Englander	Millennium Partners	230
Jeffrey Gendell	Tontine Associates	215
Kenneth Griffin	Citadel Investment Group	210
Timothy Barakett	Atticus Capital	200
William Von Mueffling	Cantillon Capital Management	200
James Pallotta	Tudor Investment Corporation	200
Raymond Dalio	Bridgewater Associates	190
John Griffin	Blue Ridge Capital	175
Louis Bacon	Moore Capital Management	160
Noam Gottesman	GLG Partners	150
Pierre Lagrange	GLG Partners	150
Daniel Loeb	Third Point	150
David Slager	Atticus Capital	150
Daniel Och	Och-Ziff Capital Management Group	145
Marc Lasry	Avenue Capital Group	130
William Browder	Hermitage Capital Management	130

Source: *Alpha*, published by *Institutional Investor*

A world of lawyers

2005	No. of lawyers	No. of lawyers as % of population
US	1,116,967*	0.373
Spain	105,000	0.248
England & Wales	126,142	0.238
Greece	25,000	0.227
Portugal	23,000	0.225
Ireland†	7,900	0.203
Scotland	9,637	0.190
Germany	116,000	0.141
Belgium	13,050	0.125
Norway	5,600	0.124
Italy	70,000	0.120
Switzerland	7,000	0.094
Denmark	4,800	0.089
Hungary	8,000	0.078
Netherlands	11,200	0.068
France	40,000	0.065
Czech Republic	6,000	0.059
Romania	13,000	0.059
Austria	4,100	0.051
Turkey	35,000	0.050
Sweden	4,100	0.047
Finland	1,700	0.033
Russia	19,000	0.013

*As of June 2006. †6,500 solicitors, 1,400 barristers.
Sources: American Bar Association; Legal 500; US Census Bureau; The Law Society of England & Wales; The Law Society of Scotland; National Statistics UK

The number of acc%untants

2001	Public practice	Business	Government	Total	No. of accountants as % of pop.
Austria	8,076	na	na	8,076	0.100
Belgium	4,659	2,329	na	6,988	0.068
Czech Republic	1,314	308	na	1,622	0.016
Denmark	1,903	785	20	2,708	0.050
Finland	1,436	62	19	1,517	0.029
France	29,614	na	na	29,614	0.050
Germany	9,047	na	na	9,047	0.011
Greece	505	na	na	505	0.005
Hungary	3,611	1,168	584	5,363	0.054
Ireland	4,675	13,280	219	18,174	0.466
Italy	88,350	1,470	980	90,800	0.158
Luxembourg	606	10	2	618	0.155
Malta	482	424	31	937	0.234
Netherlands	4,521	5,386	1,279	11,186	0.069
Norway	2,800	190	50	3,040	0.068
Poland	7,723	na	na	7,723	0.020
Portugal	899	na	na	899	0.009
Romania	9,017	na	13	9,030	0.040
Slovenia	270	177	24	471	0.024
Spain	2,829	2,447	na	5,276	0.013
Sweden	2,030	na	13	2,043	0.023
Switzerland	3,500	100	100	3,700	0.051
UK	83,948	175,178	25,003	284,129	0.481
US	na	na	na	600,000*	0.206

*Estimate.

Sources: The Federation of European Accountants; National Association of State Boards of Accountancy; UNDP, HDR

00000=-%$±/£

Women in business

Firsts among women

1809 Mary Kies – first woman to receive
a US patent (for weaving straw in hatmaking)
1963 Katharine Graham – first woman CEO in the
Fortune 500 list of US companies (The Washington Post Co)
1967 Muriel "Mickey" Siebert – first woman to purchase
a seat on the New York Stock Exchange
1997 Marjorie Scardino – first woman CEO of a FTSE 100
company (Pearson)
1999 Carly Fiorina – first woman CEO in the 30-
company Dow Jones Industrial Average (Hewlett-Packard)
2001 Clara Furse – first woman to become CEO of the
London Stock Exchange
2002 Baroness Sarah Hogg – first chairwoman of a
FTSE 100 company (3i)
2006 Bishop Katharine Jefferts Schori – first woman
leader in the Anglican church

Sources: Press reports

Most powerful women in business in America

Meg Whitman	eBay CEO
Anne Mulcahy	Xerox CEO
Brenda Barnes	Sara Lee CEO
Oprah Winfrey	Harpo chairman
Andrea Jung	Avon Products CEO
Pat Woertz	ChevronTexaco executive vice-president, Global Downstream
Sallie Krawcheck	Citigroup CFO
Abigail Johnson	Fidelity Employer Services president
Karen Katen	Pfizer executive vice-chairman; Human Health president
Judy McGrath	MTV Networks CEO

Source: *Fortune*

Most powerful women outside America

Anne Lauvergeon	Areva	France	Chairman
Xie Qihua	Shanghai Baosteel Group	China	Chairman and president
Marjorie Scardino	Pearson	UK	CEO
Linda Cook	Shell Gas & Power	Netherlands	CEO
Tomoyo Nonaka	Sanyo Electric	Japan	CEO
Marina Berlusconi	Fininvest	Italy	Vice-chairman
Nancy McKinstry	Wolters Kluwer	Netherlands	CEO
Ana Patricia Botín	Banco Banesto	Spain	Chairman
Mary Ma	Lenovo	China	CEO
Fumiko Hayashi	Daiei	Japan	CEO

Source: *Fortune*

Most powerful women working in entertainment

Anne Sweeney	The Walt Disney Company	Co-chairman of media networks; president of Disney-ABC Television Group
Judy McGrath	MTV Networks	Chairman and CEO
Stacey Snider	Universal Pictures	Chairman
Amy Pascal	Sony Pictures Entertainment	Vice-chairman
Nancy Tellem	CBS Paramount Network Television Entertainment Group	President
Gail Berman	Paramount Pictures	President
Nina Jacobson	Buena Vista Motion Pictures Group	President
Oprah Winfrey	Harpo Entertainment	Chairman
Dana Walden	20th Century Fox Television	President

Note: Most powerful women rankings are for 2005.
Source: *Hollywood Reporter*

TALL buildings

Office	Height, m	Height, ft	No. of floors	Year completed	Location
Taipei 101	509	1671	101	2004	Taipei
Petronas Tower 1	452	1483	88	1998	Kuala Lumpur
Petronas Tower 2	452	1483	88	1998	Kuala Lumpur
Sears Tower	442	1450	108	1974	Chicago
Two International Finance	415	1362	88	2003	Hong Kong
CITIC Plaza	391	1283	80	1997	Guangzhou
Shun Hing Square	384	1260	69	1996	Shenzhen
Empire State Building	381	1250	102	1931	New York City
Central Plaza	374	1227	78	1992	Hong Kong
Bank of China Tower	367	1205	72	1990	Hong Kong

Residential	Height, m	Height, ft	No. of floors	Year completed	Location
Q1 Tower	323	1058	78	2005	Gold Coast City
Eureka Tower	297	975	91	2006	Melbourne
Bright Star Tower	280	919	60	2007	Dubai
21st Century Tower	269	883	55	2003	Dubai
Triumph-Palace	264	866	54	2004	Moscow
Tower Palace Three, Tower G	264	865	73	2004	Seoul
Trump World Tower	262	861	72	2001	New York City
Sorrento 1	256	841	75	2003	Hong Kong
Emirates Marina Serviced Appartments & Spa	256	840	59	2006	Dubai
Mok-dong Hyperion I, Tower A	256	840	69	2003	Seoul

Cities with the most completed high-rise buildings*

Hong Kong	7,548	Singapore	3,693
New York City	5,489	Seoul	2,842
São Paulo	3,873	Tokyo	2,638

*Above 12 floors.
Note: Burj Dubai will be the tallest building standing at 705m (2,313ft) once completed in 2008.
Source: Emporis

BIG shopping malls

US, 2004

	Retail space, sq. feet, m	No. of shops	Location	Year opened
South Coast Plaza	2.700	280	Orange County, California	1967
Sawgrass Mills	2.503	300	Sunrise, Florida	1990
Del Amo Fashion Centre	2.500	300	Torrance, California	1975
Mall of America	2.500	428	Bloomington, Minnesota	1992
Galleria	2.400	375	Dallas, Texas	1970
Woodfield Mall	2.224	245	Chicago, Illinois	1971
Roosevelt Field Mall	2.146	220	Garden City, New York	1956
Millcreek Mall	2.139	171	Erie, Pennsylvania	1974
Lakewood Centre	2.121	255	Lakewood, California	1951
NorthPark Centre	2.100	160	Dallas, Texas	1965
Tysons Corner Centre	2.091	250	Washington, DC	1968
Oakbrook Shopping Centre	2.087	175	Oak Brook, Illinois	1962

Source: Eastern Connecticut State University, Emil Pocock

UK, 2004

	Location	Retail space*, sq metres, 000
Merry Hill	Brierley Hill	136.18
Bluewater	Kent	122.91
Metro Centre	Gateshead	122.38
Trafford Centre	Manchester	121.64
Lakeside	Essex	112.04
Meadowhall Centre	Sheffield	108.51
Braehead	Renfrew	95.78
Brent Cross	North London	57.72
Cribbs Causeway	Bristol	57.38
Edinburgh – Ocean Terminal	Edinburgh	20.23

*Not including service outlets, leisure facilities, vacants and non-selling space.
Source: Experian Business Strategies

$pending on advertising

	Total, 2005, $m	% of GDP	Per head, 2004, $
Argentina	1,148	0.70	26.1
Australia	7,476	1.14	348.5
Austria	2,585	0.85	308.1
Belgium	3,019	0.83	278.6
Brazil	6,496	0.83	25.3
Bulgaria	383	1.50	39.1
Canada	7,036	0.68	211.6
Chile	647	0.69	37.3
China	9,716	0.52	6.5
Colombia	1,287	1.25	22.8
Czech Republic	1,692	1.49	146.9
Denmark	2,072	0.82	359.5
Egypt	646	0.62	7.0
Estonia	91	0.74	58.8
Finland	1,477	0.78	272.7
France	12,658	0.61	206.2
Germany	20,235	0.73	243.4
Greece	2,741	1.25	229.5
Hong Kong	2,499	1.44	322.8
Hungary	2,481	2.29	215.8
India	3,673	0.48	2.8
Indonesia	3,055	1.04	11.9
Ireland	1,816	0.93	424.7
Israel	805	0.65	116.6
Italy	10,720	0.63	179.6
Japan	41,036	0.86	315.2
Kuwait	395	0.82	128.2
Latvia	111	0.71	39.3
Lithuania	131	0.53	35.0
Malaysia	1,199	0.94	46.8
Mexico	3,507	0.50	32.6
Netherlands	4,585	0.78	277.0
New Zealand	1,382	1.33	333.2
Norway	2,937	1.12	559.9
Panama	237	1.63	70.1

Peru	253	0.35	8.1
Philippines	646	0.68	7.1
Poland	3,507	1.37	88.2
Portugal	1,161	0.67	108.0
Puerto Rico	1,831	2.26	485.9
Romania	306	0.41	11.8
Russia	5,010	0.81	27.2
Saudi Arabia/			
Pan Arab	2,823	1.05	102.8
Singapore	1,240	1.11	281.7
South Africa	2,643	1.15	50.3
South Korea	6,912	0.95	142.7
Spain	8,265	0.74	179.2
Sweden	2,369	0.67	250.0
Switzerland	3,042	0.83	404.7
Taiwan	1,722	0.52	77.4
Thailand	2,272	1.28	33.0
Turkey	1,499	0.48	17.9
UK	21,338	0.96	347.4
Uruguay	56	0.40	14.0
US	166,235	1.33	546.7
Venezuela	576	0.51	21.9
Vietnam	334	0.64	3.2
Total	396,989	0.96	81.2

Source: ZenithOptimedia

%	Television	Newspapers	Magazines	Radio	Out-of-home	Internet	Cinema
2004	37.6	30.2	13.6	8.7	5.8	3.7	0.4
2005	37.2	30.0	13.4	8.5	5.9	4.6	0.4
2006	37.3	29.4	13.2	8.4	6.0	5.4	0.4
2007	37.3	28.8	13.1	8.3	6.1	6.0	0.4
2008	37.6	28.2	12.9	8.2	6.3	6.4	0.4

Note: 2005 is estimate; 2006–08 are forecasts.
Source: ZenithOptimedia

Some famous advertising slogans

"All the news that's fit to print." *New York Times* (1896)

"Good to the last drop." Maxwell House coffee (1915)

"I'd walk a mile for a Camel." Camel (1921)

"Ask the man who owns one." Packard (1925)

"Guinness is good for you." Guinness (1929)

"Snap! Crackle! Pop!" Kellogg's Rice Krispies (1932)

"Don't be vague. Ask for Haig." Haig Scotch Whisky (1934)

"If you want to get ahead, get a hat." Hat Council (1934)

"Careless Talk Costs Lives." UK Ministry of Information (1940)

"Think." IBM (1941)

"A diamond is forever." De Beers (1948)

"Drink a pinta milka day." National Milk Publicity Council (1958)

"A little dab'll do ya." Brylcreem (1949)

"Finger lickin' good." Kentucky Fried Chicken (1952)

"The milk chocolate melts in your mouth, not in your hand." M&Ms (1954)

"You'll wonder where the yellow went when you brush your teeth with Pepsodent." Pepsodent (1956)

"Go to work on an egg." UK Egg Marketing Board (1957)

"Happiness is a cigar called Hamlet." Hamlet (1960)

"Think small." Volkswagen (1962)

"We try harder." Avis (1962)

"Schhh … You-Know-Who." Schweppes (1962)

"Put a tiger in your tank" Esso (1964)

"Let your fingers do the walking." Yellow Pages (1964)

"A Mars a day helps you work, rest and play." Mars (1965)

"Beanz Meanz Heinz." Heinz (1967)

"Because I'm worth it." L'Oréal (1967)

"Say it with flowers" Interflora (1971)

"Accountancy was my life until I discovered Smirnoff." Smirnoff (1971)

"Probably the best beer in the world." Carlsberg (1973)

"Lipsmackin' thirstquenchin' acetastin' motivatin' goodbuzzin' cooltalkin' highwalkin' fastlivin' evergivin' coolfizzin' Pepsi." Pepsi Cola (1973)

"Heineken refreshes the parts other beers cannot reach." Heineken (1974)

"For mash get Smash." Smash instant mashed potatoes (1974)

"Don't leave home without it." American Express (1975)

"The ultimate driving machine." BMW (1975)

"Reach out and touch someone." AT&T (1979)

"I liked it so much I bought the company." Remington shavers (1979)

"H2Eau." Perrier (1980)

"Reassuringly expensive." Stella Artois (1981)

"When it absolutely, positively, has to be there overnight." Federal Express (1982)

"The world's favourite airline." British Airways (1983)

"Vorsprung durch technik." Audi (1984)

"Australians wouldn't give a Castlemaine XXXX for anything else." (1986)

"Just do it." Nike (1988)

"It's everywhere you want to be." Visa (1988)

"Intel inside." Intel (1990)

"It's good to talk." British Telecom (1994)

"The future's bright. The future's Orange." Orange (1996)

"Absolut perfection." Absolut Vodka (1998)

"Think different." Apple Macintosh (1998)

"Be the first to know." CNN (2002)

"10,000 songs in your pocket." iPod (2004)

"Buy it. Sell it. Love it." Ebay (2005)

"So where the bloody hell are you?" Australian Tourist Commission (2006)

Some business **giants** of the past

Carnegie, Andrew (1835–1919)

The richest man ever to come out of Dumfermline, Andrew Carnegie left Scotland for Pittsburgh, Pennsylvania, with his family in search of work after the introduction of the mechanical loom put his weaver father out of work. Carnegie's first job was as a bobbin boy in a textile factory. After later jobs as a clerk and a messenger boy, in 1853 he became assistant to Tom Scott, the superintendent of the Pennsylvania Railroad's western division. He started investing on his own behalf in iron manufacturing and other businesses, and made substantial returns. In 1859 he was promoted to the position of superintendent and in 1865 he resigned from the railroad to concentrate on business, in particular iron and steel. The civil war had fuelled demand for iron, as had the move to replace wooden bridges with iron ones and, most important of all, the expansion of the railroads. Carnegie introduced the Bessemer steel process to America, which meant that steel could be produced at greater speed and lower cost, with the result that the Carnegie Steel Company was producing a quarter of America's steel by 1900 and was making a profit of $40m. Carnegie believed that great wealth was of no value unless it was put to good use and he wrote several treatises on this theme, including the *Gospel of Wealth* in which he argued that any riches beyond those needed for the survival of one's family should be used for the good of the wider community. By the time he sold his company to J.P. Morgan in 1901 for $480m, Carnegie had already spent a great deal of money in accordance with his principles. As a self-educated but cultivated man, he was a great believer in public libraries and he spent over $50m

> **❝Carnegie believed that great wealth was of no value unless it was put to good use❞**

setting up some 2,500 of them. By the time he died, he
had given away $350m.

Disney, Walt Elias (1901–66)

Walt Disney was a sentimentalist whose somewhat rigid
idea of America on occasions gave his work a sinister edge.
The inventor and voice of Mickey Mouse also produced
cheery military propaganda like *Victory Through Airpower*
and in 1947 appeared before the House Committee on
Un-American Activities to name employees he said were
communist infiltrators: "I really feel that they ought to be
smoked out for what they are so that all the liberalisms
that really are American can go out without the taint of
communism." Between 1942 and 1943, 95% of Disney
Studios' output was on contract to the US government
and Disney was particularly proud of his contribution to
the tax-take after *The New Spirit* explained the importance
of declaring your income for tax.

He was born in Chicago, left school to drive an
ambulance for the Red Cross in France aged 16 and
returned from there, having survived influenza in the
great epidemic, in 1919. Walt began drawing cartoons
and set up a little company, Laugh-O-Gram Films, before
moving to Hollywood. There he
brought Oswald the Lucky Rabbit
into existence and then Mickey
Mouse, who appeared with
synchronised sound. Walt Disney was among the first to
recognise the importance of sound for bringing cartoons,
and later nature films, to life. He also pioneered
Technicolor, winning an Academy Award for *Flowers and
Trees* in 1932. The combination of these successes led to a
feature-length cartoon and *Snow White and the Seven
Dwarves* opened in 1937. The profits ran to millions and
Disney set about constructing $3m offices that would
churn out the now familiar Disney cartoons.
He returned to bulk-making cartoons after the war, but

> **Walt was among
> the first to recognise the
> importance of sound**

some business giants of the past *continued*

also continued with informational films such as those about NASA which he made with the help of ex-Nazi Wernher von Braun, inventor of the V2 Rocket. Disneyland opened in 1955 in Anaheim, California, and there were other theme-parks on the horizon. These perhaps helped formulate an idea in Walt's mind that he called EPCOT (Experimental Prototype Community of Tomorrow). But he died before he was able to see its fruition.

Ford, Henry (1863–1947)

Henry Ford is best known for the invention of the Model T Ford and the moving assembly line and less well-known as the US publisher of the notorious anti-semitic *Protocols of the Elders of Zion* (in his newspaper *The Dearborn Independent*). Ford was born to Irish immigrant parents from County Cork and left the family farm to work as a machinist in Detroit. He returned to work on the family farm in 1882 but was shortly afterwards taken on, thanks to his skills with steam engines, as a maintenance engineer in a local company. In 1891 he joined the Edison Illuminating Company but found sufficient spare time to invent, build and drive his Quadricycle which led to the creation of the Henry Ford Company. This, however, was taken over by the investors who turned it into Cadillac, so Henry Ford set up the Ford motor company in 1903 and released the Model T six years later. In 1918, half of all cars in America were Model T Fords. Ford's approach to his workers was paternalistic but combined the generous treatment of suitable workers with suppression of union activity.

Gibbs, William (1790–1875)

"Mr Gibbs made his tibbs selling turds of foreign birds." One of the sons of Anthony Gibbs, William built churches and the grand house of Tyntesfield near Bristol with money made from guano. Guano is seabird dung, rich in nitrates and phosphates, and was harvested in earnest off South America's coast from the middle of the 19th century as fertiliser. William and his brother George signed their first contract with the Peruvian government in 1842 and in 1858 imported 300,000 tons of guano to Britain. William was able to build Tyntesfield at a cost of £70,000, the profits of just one year's trade. (In 2002 the house was acquired by the National Trust for £25m.) He also paid for churches to be built elsewhere, including the chapel of Keble College, Oxford.

Ray Kroc (1902–84)

It was Ray Kroc who persuaded Dick and Mac McDonald to expand and set up their restaurants across the United States, and to employ him to oversee this project. At the age of 15, Ray Kroc, who had lied about his age, had been destined for Europe as a Red Cross ambulance driver. He was saved by the war ending before he could leave and began instead a variety of salesman's jobs. He first met the McDonald brothers when selling mixing machines for restaurants; their purchase of eight of these machines gave him the idea for setting up identikit restaurants like theirs. Kroc prided himself on his standards of quality, service and cleanliness, and he believed that there should be no reservations, no waiting and low prices. There was no doubt, however, about his core principle – in his own words: "The definition of salesmanship is the gentle art of letting the customer have it your way." He was chairman of the McDonald's Corporation from its creation in 1955 until his death and he never stopped developing new ideas, from German taverns to theme parks. When his widow, Joan, died in 2004, she left a bequest of £800m to the Salvation Army.

> **salesmanship is the gentle art of letting the customer have it *your* way**

some business **giants** of the past *continued*

Krupp, Alfred (1812–87)

Alfred Krupp was an outstanding businessman and engineer who profited from industrialisation and war in Europe. Born in Essen into a family of metal-workers, he began work in the family iron forge when his father fell ill. Together with his mother, who took control of the firm on the death of her husband in 1826, Alfred began building on the possibilities presented by the manufacture of steel. The firm became a central element in the building of the railways and produced, among other railway components, the seamless wheel tyre. Increasingly, however, Alfred was looking to armaments for the company's survival – he had produced its first steel gun in 1847. In 1848, he became the head of the company and began in earnest the acquisition of mines, docks and collieries in order to guarantee the raw materials that he needed. By the time of his death, Krupps employed 20,200 people and had instituted a rule that the company could only be passed to a single heir. Later, the Krupps firm would produce the artillery used to shell Paris in first world war ("Big Bertha"). The Krupp whose collaboration with Adolf Hitler led to the break-up of the Krupp empire was in fact Gustav von Bohlen und Halbach, who changed his name when he married Alfred's granddaughter, Bertha.

William Hesketh Lever (1851–1925)

Born in Bolton in the north of England, Lever was a pioneering manufacturer of soap who applied his wealth to a variety of good causes. In 1886, he was the founding partner in Lever Brothers with James Lever. In the course of their business, they made the discovery that soap could be made from vegetable oil instead of tallow and from that discovery came Sunlight soap – hence Port Sunlight, the model village near Liverpool that Lever built for his workers. After his purchase of the Scottish islands of Harris and Lewis in 1918, he established similar projects there, too, and spent large sums of money trying to create a gainfully employed community free from poverty. Lever is known for his art collections, which served a dual purpose, for not only did he have a passion for art and artefacts, but he also saw that certain types of painting could be used to promote soap sales. These tended to be illustrations of pristine clothes worn by happy but poor people. The artists were not always happy to find their creations used in this way. However, after his wife's death in 1913, Lever built a gallery in her memory where the pictures and other collections are preserved. Lever's pre-eminence in business and social zeal were recognised by a series of titles. He was MP for the Wirral and was made a baronet. He was raised to the peerage as Lord Leverhulme of Bolton-le-Moors in 1917 and became Viscount Leverhulme of the Isles five years later. To this day, money left by him is given to research and education projects.

" he saw that certain types of painting could be used to promote soap sales "

Morgan, John Pierpoint (1837–1913)

The richest man in America by 1900, John Pierpoint Morgan made his money through the financing of debt and the control of important US industries. He rescued America's finances on more than one occasion, notably helping to refinance the civil war debt and bailing out Wall Street during its financial crisis in 1907. Born into a banking family, Morgan travelled widely when he was young and graduated from the University of Göttingen. After a stretch working as an accountant for the Duncan Sherman & Co banking house, he began working in as an accountant for a finance house that served George Peabody, his father's partner, in New York. His father, Junius Spencer, subsequently succeeded Peabody and

some business **giants** of the past *continued*

renamed the company J.S. Morgan, which John Pierpoint joined in 1864. In 1895, he took over the bank, and it became J.P. Morgan. He began systematising the railroads and gained stock in the railroad companies he reorganised; by 1900 he controlled 5,000 miles of railroad rights, one-sixth of the total. There followed the purchase and consolidation of US steel manufacturing – he bought the Carnegie Steel Company from Andrew Carnegie for $480m and joined it to his own Federal Steel Company in

❝he rescued America's finances on more than one occasion❞

1901. The resulting US Steel Corporation was the first company in the world to be capitalised at over $1 billion. In the meantime, he had also

started the International Harvester Company, which dealt in agricultural equipment, and the International Mercantile Marine shipping company (owner of White Star Line, which built the Titanic). It was with reason that antitrust campaigners attacked him given that he controlled several industries almost in their entirety. In spite of the cathedral and churches he built, and his intervention to save Wall Street in 1907 (which eventually led to the creation of the Federal Reserve System), J.P. Morgan's reputation still hangs somewhere between "robber baron" and builder of America's economy.

Morita, Akio (1921–99)

The man who conceived the idea of the Walkman was born into a Nagoya family that traded in sake and soy sauce. Instead of working in the family firm and ignoring his father's advice that he study economics, Morita chose to study electronics at Tokyo University. It was in his subsequent work in missile design that he met Masaru Ibuka with whom, in 1946, he set up Tokyo

Telecommunications and Engineering Industries (Tokyo Tsushin Kogyo). Masaru was the source of much of the company's electrical engineering success but Morita provided the business sense that underlay the greatest achievements. He wanted to destroy the image of Japan as a source of cheap and shoddy goods and started selling the company's products abroad. In 1958 he rebranded the company as Sony (a combination of *sonus* (Latin: sound) and Sonny Boy), and in 1961 Sony was the first foreign company to be listed on the New York Stock Exchange. Morita retired from Sony in 1994. Henry Kissinger said that he was probably the most effective spokesman for Japan he ever met.

Rockefeller, John Davison (1839–1937)

The wealth of the Rockefellers was created by John Davison Rockefeller through control of oil production in the United States. He began as a book-keeper in a company buying and selling futures and then moved to an oil refinery in Ohio. In 1870, with several others, Rockefeller founded Standard Oil. The company grew in power through the acquisition of competing refineries and through control of the railroads. The scale of consolidation was such that Standard Oil came under attack from the antitrust movement and in

> **❝one of the great philanthopists, he had given away $500 million by the time he died❞**

1911 was ordered by the US Supreme Court to be broken up; many new small companies were formed from its ruins. But the Rockefeller fortune had been made. John Rockefeller was reckoned to be worth $900m in 1901 and, one of the modern age's great philanthropists, had given away $500m by the time he died; he had founded the University of Chicago, the Rockefeller Institute for Medical Research and The Rockefeller Foundation to "promote the well-being of mankind" and had supported many other organisations and institutions. It was his son,

some business giants of the past *continued*

John Davison Rockefeller II, who built the Rockefeller Centre in New York.

Woolworth, Frank (1852–1919)

Frank Woolworth originally conceived the idea of selling goods at discounted and fixed prices when he observed the attraction discount stalls of leftovers held for customers. He reasoned that this was because of the price but also because people liked seeing and handling the goods. On this basis he set up the first of his stores in 1879. His misjudgment on this occasion was to sell goods at only five cents and the shop went bust.

> **his misjudgment on this occasion was to sell goods at only five cents and the shop went bust**

Undeterred, he proceeded to set up new stores which offered goods at both five and ten cents (hence "five and ten cents stores"). After one or two further failures the business started to grow, and by 1904 there were 120 Woolworths stores in 21 states across America. On his death in 1919, Woolworth had established more than 1,000 stores in America and elsewhere and a $65m corporation had been formed. Woolworth built the eponymous tower in New York which was the tallest in the world at the time.

Some management styles

Management by exception – the policy of only looking closely at events that deviate significantly from an expected norm; for example, a drop in more than a certain percentage in sales revenue or a payment that is more than a specified number of days overdue.

Management by objectives – used to describe a management system whereby employees agree with their managers what their objectives are to be and then track progress in moving towards those objectives with their managers.

Management by walking about – most famously demonstrated by Hewlett-Packard, a computer firm, management by walking about is a style of management that emphasises the importance of face-to-face contact.

Managerial grid – a way to classify managerial styles by plotting "concern for results" against "concern for people", each on a scale of 1–9. For example:

1,1 the impoverished style – only concerned to get the necessary work done with the minimum effort

9,1 the scientific management style – where there is a concentration on maximising efficiency

5,5 the middle of the road style – where the aim is to get reasonable results and keep people reasonably happy

9,9 the team management style – where everyone works together to get the best out of themselves and others.

Philanthr💚py

America's most generous philanthropists

	Background	2001–05 given or pledged, $bn
Gordon & Betty Moore	Intel co-founder	7.05
Bill & Melinda Gates	Microsoft co-founder	5.46
Warren Buffett	Berkshire Hathaway CEO	2.62
George Soros	Investor	2.37
Eli & Edythe Broad	SunAmerica, KB Home founder	1.48
James & Virginia Stowers	American Century founder	1.21
Walton Family	Family of Wal-Mart founder	1.10
Alfred Mann	Medical devices	0.99
Michael & Susan Dell	Dell founder	0.93
George Kaiser	Oil and gas, banking, real estate	0.62
John Templeton	Investor	0.56
Ruth Lilly	Eli Lilly heiress	0.56
Michael Bloomberg	Bloomberg founder, NYC mayor	0.53
Veronica Atkins	Widow of Dr Atkins	0.50

Source: *BusinessWeek*

Britain's most generous philanthropists

2006*	Background	Wealth, £m
Robert Edmiston	Car sales and property	410
Sir Tom Hunter	Sports goods and investments	780
Sir Elton John	Music	205
George Weston	Food production	932
Leo Noe	Property	380
Lord Sainsbury	Supermarkets	1,600
Johan Eliasch	Sports goods and investments	361
Everard Goodman	Property	140

*Year to April.
†Recent donations as % of net wealth.
Source: *Sunday Times*

Causes	Estimated lifetime giving, $bn	Donations as % of net worth
Environment, science	7.30	159
Health, education, libraries	27.98	55
Reproductive choice, reducing nukes	2.73	7
Open and democratic societies	5.40	75
Public education, arts, science	1.82	33
Biomedical research	1.58	220
Education	1.35	2
Biomedical education and research	1.50	71
Children's health and education	1.23	7
Anti-poverty in Oklahoma	0.72	16
Spirituality and science	1.00	50
Poetry, libraries, culture, scholarships	0.76	362
Education, health care, arts	0.73	14
Eradication of obesity and diabetes	0.50	1,000

Causes	Recent donations £m	Giving index†
Religious, humanitarian, education	43.7	10.67
Humanitarian, education, children	78.3	10.03
AIDS, medical, children, football, music	20.5	10.00
Education, medical, social, arts, religion	69.9	7.50
Education, religious, humanitarian	27.1	7.13
Education, medical, arts, humanitarian	102.1	6.38
Environmental	22.5	6.23
Education, medical	5.0	3.56

The richest people

World, 1996

	Worth, $bn	Country/region
Bill Gates	18.5	US
Warren Buffett	15.0	US
Paul Sacher, Oeri & Hoffmann, family	13.1	Switzerland
Lee Shau Kee	12.7	Hong Kong
Tsai Wan-lin, family	12.2	Taiwan
Kwok, Brothers	11.2	Hong Kong
Li Ka-shing, family	10.6	Hong Kong
Yoshiaki Tsutsumi	9.2	Japan
Theo & Karl Albrecht	9.0	Germany
Hans & Gad Rausing	9.0	Scandinavia
Johanna, Susanne & Stefan Quandt	8.1	Germany
Haniel, family	8.1	Germany
Paul Allen	7.5	US

World, 2005

	Worth, $bn	Country/region
Bill Gates	50.0	US
Warren Buffett	42.0	US
Carlos Slim Helu	30.0	Mexico
Ingvar Kamprad	28.0	Sweden
Lakshmi Mittal	23.5	India
Paul Allen	22.0	US
Bernard Arnault	21.5	France
Prince Alwaleed Bin Talal Alsaud	20.0	Saudi Arabia
Kenneth Thomson & family	19.6	Canada
Li Ka-shing	18.8	Hong Kong
Roman Abramovich	18.2	Russia
Michael Dell	17.1	US
Karl Albrecht	17.0	Germany
Sheldon Adelson	16.1	US
Liliane Bettencourt	16.0	France

Source: *Forbes*

Europe's richest people

2006	£bn	Country of residence
Karl & Theo Albrecht *	18.4	Germany
Ingvar Kamprad	16.0	Sweden
Lakshmi Mittal	14.9	UK
Bernard Arnault	12.3	France
Johanna Quandt *	11.9	Germany
Roman Abramovich	10.8	UK
Liliane Bettencourt	9.1	France
Amancio Ortega	8.5	Spain
The Herz family	7.4	Germany
The Brenninkmeyer family	7.1	Holland
Stefan Persson	7.0	Sweden
The Mulliez family	6.9	France
The Oeri/Hoffmann family	6.8	Switzerland
Adolf Merckle	6.6	Germany
Duke of Westminster	6.6	UK
Vagit Alekperov	6.3	Russia
Silvio Berlusconi	6.3	Italy
Vladimir Lisin	6.1	Russia
Michael Otto *	5.9	Germany
Luciano Benetton *	5.8	Italy
Michele Ferrero *	5.7	Italy
Leonardo Del Vecchio	5.7	Italy
Viktor Vekselberg	5.7	Russia
Mikhail Fridman	5.5	Russia
Spiro Latsis *	5.2	Greece
Serge Dassault *	4.9	France
Philip & Tina Green	4.9	UK
Birgit Rausing *	4.9	Switzerland/UK
Hans Rausing *	4.9	UK
Hilary Weston *	4.8	Canada/Ireland

Note: *denotes family wealth.
Source: *Sunday Times*

Central bankers since 1900

Bank of England governors

	Year appointed
Samuel Steuart Gladstone	1899
Sir Augustus Prevost	1901
Samuel Hope Morley	1903
Alexander Falconer Wallace	1905
William Middleton Campbell	1907
Reginald Eden Johnston	1909
Alfred Clayton Cole	1911
Walter Cunliffe	1913
Sir Brien Ibrican Cokayne	1918
Montagu Collet Norman	1920
Lord Catto of Cairncatto	1944
Cameron Fromanteel Cobbold	1949
The Earl of Cromer	1961
Leslie Kenneth O'Brien	1966
Gordon William Humphreys Richardson	1973
Robert (Robin) Leigh-Pemberton	1983
Edward Alan John George	1993
Mervyn Allister King	2003

US Federal Reserve chairmen

	Year appointed
Charles S. Hamlin	1914
W. P. G. Harding	1916
Daniel R Crissinger	1923
Roy A. Young	1927
Eugene Meyer	1930
Eugene R. Black	1933
Marriner S. Eccles	1934
Thomas B. McCabe	1948
Wm McC Martin, Jr	1951
Arthur F. Burns	1970
G. William Miller	1978
Paul A. Volcker	1979
Alan Greenspan	1987
Ben S. Bernanke	2006

European Central Bank presidents

	Year appointed
Willem F. Duisenberg	1998
Jean-Claude Trichet	2003

Bank of Japan presidents

	Year appointed
Tatsuo Yamamoto	1898
Baron Shigeyoshi Matsuo	1903
Korekiyo Takahashi	1911
Viscount Yataro Mishima	1913
Junnosuke Inoue	1919
Otohiko Ichiki	1923
Junnosuke Inoue	1927
Hisaakira Hijikata	1928
Eigo Fukai	1935
Seihin Ikeda	1937
Toyotaro Yuki	1937
Viscount Keizo Shibusawa	1944
Eikichi Araki	1945
Hisato Ichimada	1946
Eikichi Araki	1954
Masamichi Yamagiwa	1956
Makoto Usami	1964
Tadashi Sasaki	1969
Teiichiro Morinaga	1974
Haruo Mayekawa	1979
Satoshi Sumita	1984
Yasushi Mieno	1989
Yasuo Matsushita	1994
Masaru Hayami	1998
Toshihiko Fukui	2003

Sources: Central banks

"In their own words"

■ Business is really more agreeable than pleasure; it interests the whole mind … more deeply. But it does not look as if it did.
Walter Bagehot, English journalist and author and early editor of *The Economist*

■ We don't have a monopoly. We have market share. There's a difference.
Steve Ballmer, CEO of Microsoft

■ Every young man would do well to remember that all successful business stands on the foundation of morality.
Henry Ward Beecher, 19th century American theologian

■ Failing organisations are usually over-managed and under-led.
Warren G. Bennis, management theorist

■ The economic repercussions of a stockmarket crash depend less on the severity of the crash itself than on the response of economic policymakers, particularly central bankers.
Ben Bernanke, Chairman of the Federal Reserve

■ A brand for a company is like a reputation for a person. You earn reputation by trying to do hard things well.
Jeff Bezos, founder of Amazon

■ The gambling known as business looks with austere disfavour upon the business known as gambling.
Ambrose Bierce, American satirist

■ Corporation: An ingenious device for obtaining profit without individual responsibility.
Ambrose Bierce

■ If you can run one business well, you can run any business well.
Sir Richard Branson, founder of Virgin group

- The market, like the Lord, helps those who help themselves. But unlike the Lord, the market does not forgive those who know not what they do.

    Warren Buffett, American investor

- I don't try to jump over seven-foot bars. I look for one-foot bars that I can step over.

    Warren Buffett

- Wide diversification is only required when investors do not understand what they are doing.

    Warren Buffett

- In the search for companies to acquire we adopt the same attitude one might find appropriate in looking for a spouse: it pays to be active, interested and open minded, but it does not pay to be in a hurry.

    ❝ ...but it does not pay to be in a _hurry_ ❞

    Warren Buffett

- Some regard private enterprise as if it were a predatory tiger to be shot. Others look upon it as a cow that they can milk. Only a handful see it for what it really is – the strong horse that pulls the whole cart.

    Winston Churchill, British statesman

- The chief business of the American people is business.

    Calvin Coolidge, former American president

- Wherever you see a successful business, someone once made a courageous decision.

    Peter Drucker, American management theorist

- Most of what we call management consists of making it difficult for people to get their work done.

    Peter Drucker

- The fewer data needed, the better the information. And an overload of information, that is, anything much beyond what is truly needed, leads to information blackout. It does not enrich, but impoverishes.

    Peter Drucker

"in their own words" *continued*

■ There is an enormous number of managers who have retired on the job.

Peter Drucker

■ The movie business has always been like the wild-catting oil business. Everyone wants a gusher.

Michael Eisner, former head of Walt Disney

■ When you innovate, you've got to be prepared for everyone telling you you're nuts.

Larry Ellison, CEO of Oracle

■ Ask five economists and you'll get five different answers – six if one went to Harvard.

Edgar Fiedler, economist

■ Once I began following my own instincts, sales took off and I became a millionaire. And that, I think, is a key secret to every person's success, be they male or female, banker or pornographer: trust in your gut.

Larry Flynt, pioneering American pornographer

■ A business that makes nothing but money is a poor business.

Henry Ford, American carmaker

■ A bank is a place where they lend you an umbrella in fair weather and ask for it back when it begins to rain.

Robert Frost, American poet

■ By working faithfully eight hours a day you may eventually get to be boss and work twelve hours a day.

Robert Frost

■ Your most unhappy customers are your greatest source of learning.

Bill Gates, founder of Microsoft

■ In this business, by the time you realise you're in trouble, it's too late to save yourself. Unless you're running scared all the time, you're gone.

Bill Gates

■ The difference between tax avoidance and tax evasion is the thickness of a prison wall.

Denis Healey, British politician

■ In the end, all business operations can be reduced to three words: people, product, and profits.

Lee Iacocca, former CEO of Chrysler

■ Sometimes when you innovate, you make mistakes. It is best to admit them quickly, and get on with improving your other innovations.

Steve Jobs, founder of Apple Computer

■ Markets can remain irrational longer than you can remain solvent.

John Maynard Keynes, economist

■ Never be frightened to take a profit. Better in your pocket than theirs.

Michael Levy, American author

■ Business, more than any other occupation, is a continual dealing with the future; it is a continual calculation, an instinctive exercise in foresight.

Henry Luce, American publisher

■ There are four things that hold back human progress: ignorance, stupidity, committees and accountants.

Sir Charles Lyall, British Orientalist and civil servant

■ If you know why you bought a stock in the first place, you'll automatically have a better idea of when to say goodbye to it.

Peter Lynch, American investor

■ Business is a combination of war and sport.

Andre Maurois, French author

"in their own words" continued

■ The buck stops with the guy who signs the cheques.

Rupert Murdoch, Australian-born media magnate

■ The secret of business is to know something that nobody else knows.

Aristotle Onassis, Greek shipping tycoon

■ We don't have as many managers as we should but we would rather have too few than too many.

Larry Page, co-founder of Google

■ I am grateful for all my problems. I became stronger and more able to meet those that were still to come.

J.C. Penney, American retail pioneer

■ An economist is an expert who will know tomorrow why the things he predicted yesterday didn't happen today.

Laurence Peter, Canadian academic and humourist

■ Almost all quality improvement comes via simplification of design, manufacturing, layout, processes, and procedures.

Tom Peters, management guru

■ A friendship founded on business is a good deal better than a business founded on friendship.

John D. Rockefeller, American oilman

■ Good management consists in showing average people how to do the work of superior people.

John D. Rockefeller

■ The secret of success is to get up early, work late and strike oil.

John D. Rockefeller

■ If advertisers spent the same amount of money on improving their products as they do on advertising then they wouldn't have to advertise them.

Will Rogers, American humourist

■ If all the economists were laid end to end, they'd never reach a conclusion.

George Bernard Shaw, Irish playwright

■ It's a very sobering feeling to be up in space and realise that one's safety factor was determined by the lowest bidder on a government contract.

Alan Shepherd, American astronaut

■ The work of the individual still remains the spark that moves mankind ahead even more than teamwork.

Igor Sikorsky, Russian-born aviation pioneer

■ It's not whether you are right or wrong that's important, but how much money you make when you're right and how much you lose when you're wrong.

George Soros, Hungarian-born financier and philanthropist

■ If you don't do it excellently, don't do it at all. Because if it's not excellent, it won't be profitable or fun, and if you're not in business for fun or profit, what the hell are you doing there?

Robert Townsend, American businessman

■ Sometimes your best investments are the ones you don't make.

Donald Trump, American businessman

■ My son is now an "entrepreneur". That's what you're called when you don't have a job.

Ted Turner, founder of CNN

■ Do something. Either lead, follow or get out of the way.

Ted Turner

■ There is only one boss. The customer. And he can fire everybody in the company from the chairman on down, simply by spending his money somewhere else.

Sam Walton, founder of Wal-Mart

"in their own words" *continued*

■ Making money is art and working is art and good business is the best art.

Andy Warhol, artist

■ An organisation's ability to learn, and translate that learning into action rapidly, is the ultimate competitive advantage.

Jack Welch, former CEO of GE

■ My main job was developing talent. I was a gardener providing water and other nourishment to our top 750 people. Of course, I had to pull out some weeds, too.

Jack Welch

■ In modern business it is not the crook who is to be feared most, it is the honest man who doesn't know what he is doing.

William Wordsworth, English poet

Bad boys – and something fishy

Ivan Boesky, an American arbitrageur, coined the phrase
"greed is good" that symbolised the ethos of many of
those working in the financial markets during the 1980s.
Mr Boesky made his cash betting on corporate takeovers
but he did not rely on luck and judgment alone. He was
convicted of insider dealing, a crime often overlooked in
those freewheeling days on Wall Street, yet the blatancy
of his actions earned him three-and-a-half years in prison
and a fine of $100m even after plea bargaining and
informing on many of his sources.

Alan Bond emigrated to Australia from Britain in 1950
beginning his career as a signwriter. He built up the Perth-
based Bond Corporation making a fortune in property
development before branching out into brewing, gold
mining and television. In 1983 he made himself a
national hero by financing Australia's successful attempt
to wrest the America's Cup yachting trophy from
America, which had held it since 1851. Mr Bond used his
considerable fortune to buy significant artworks but in
1987, after buying Van Gogh's "Irises" for $54 million,
using a loan from Sotheby's, an auctioneer, things began
to go wrong. He refused to repay the loan and a
stockmarket crash exposed the weakness of his businesses
and led to bankruptcy and disgrace. In 1996 he was
sentenced to three years for fraud for selling a Manet
painting owned by the Bond Corporation to a family firm
for well below market value. In 1997 he got seven years
for diverting cash from a public company he ran to prop
up another family business. In prison he took up art.

Bernie Cornfeld, a social worker turned mutual-fund
salesman, decided to start his own operation in the 1960s.
Investors Overseas Services (IOS) was based in Geneva to
escape regulation and targeted ex-pat Americans seeking
to avoid income tax, although about half of his investors

bad boys continued

were German, also lured by his pitch – "Do you seriously want to be rich?". After ten years, IOS had raised $2.5 billion and had 1m shareholders. IOS, in effect a glorified Ponzi scheme (see Charles Ponzi below), collapsed in 1970. Cornfeld spent 11 months in a Swiss jail before fraud charges were finally dropped.

Bernie Ebbers, a cowboy-hat and boot wearing businessman and former night-club bouncer, built WorldCom from modest beginnings into a telecoms firm worth over $175 billion at the height of the stockmarket boom by relentlessly acquiring assets. In 1998, he masterminded a $37 billion merger with MCI, one of America's leading long-distance phone companies. But as the dotcom boom ran out of steam, WorldCom resorted to accounting tricks to maintain the appearance of ever-growing profitability. The fraud failed to keep the company afloat. In April 2002, Mr Ebbers was forced to step down as chief executive and later the firm admitted an $11 billion accounting fraud, resulting in America's biggest-ever bankruptcy. In 2004, Mr Ebbers was found guilty of fraud, conspiracy and filing false documents with regulators, and was sentenced in July 2005 to 25 years in jail.

Enron became one of the world's largest energy firms by trading electricity and natural gas. It had stakes in nearly 30,000 miles of gas pipeline and a 15,000-mile fibre-optic cable network. In 1999, it launched a plan to buy and sell access to high-speed internet bandwidth as well as EnronOnline, a web-based commodity-trading site, making it an e-commerce company. The company reported revenues of $101 billion in 2000 and its stock hit a record high of $90. But in October 2001 Enron reported a $638m third-quarter loss and admitted that the Securities and Exchange Commission had launched a formal investigation into a possible conflict of interest related to the company's dealings with its partners. The next month Enron revised its financial statements for the past five years to account for further losses. Enron shares plunged below $1 and in December it filed for bankruptcy protection. A congressional investigation later concluded that Enron had set up an array of dizzyingly complex schemes to hoodwink the Internal Revenue Service and enrich its executives through tricky accounting off-balance-sheet deals and tax avoidance scams. Enron management created a virtual company with virtual profits. Sixteen former Enron executives have pleaded guilty to various crimes. Andrew Fastow pleaded guilty to fraud and agreed to co-operate with

> **Enron management created a virtual company with virtual profits**

prosecutors in return for a ten-year sentence. In December 2005, Richard Causey, the firm's former chief accounting officer, pleaded guilty to securities fraud. But for prosecutors the greatest prize was the conviction of Jeffey Skilling and Kenneth Lay, the firm's two top bosses, in May 2006 after a 16-week trial. Mr Lay was found guilty of six counts of conspiracy and fraud, and Mr Skilling was found guilty on 18 counts but was acquitted on all but one charge of insider trading. In a separate trial in front of the judge, Mr Lay was also found guilty of bank fraud. Both faced very long sentences but Mr Lay died in July 2006 before sentence had been passed.

Martin Frankel, an American money manager, was arrested in Germany in 1999 after an international manhunt. He was reportedly in possession of nine fake passports, 547 diamonds, an astrological chart drawn up to answer the question "Will I go to prison?" and a to-do list that included "launder money". In 2002, Mr Frankel pleaded guilty to 24 federal corruption charges for defrauding more than $200m from insurance companies in the southern United States. His technique was to buy

bad boys *continued*

small insurance firms and help himself to their assets in order to fund his lavish lifestyle. He was sentenced to 17 years in prison in 2004.

Kim Woo Choong, founder of South Korea's Daewoo, was held in high esteem for building his small textile-trading house into one of the country's largest industrial conglomerates. The business reached from automobiles and electronics to financial services and construction. After the Asian financial crisis of 1997, the firm struggled to repay huge sums borrowed to finance expansion and the group collapsed in 1999 with debts of some $70 billion. After seven of Mr Kim's top aides were arrested on charges of fraud and embezzlement, Mr Kim went on the run. He is thought to have nipped between Europe and Africa to avoid prosecution on similar charges of running a massive accounting fraud to prop up his ailing business. Mr Kim returned to South Korea in 2005 to face justice. The 69-year-old was found guilty of embezzlement and accounting fraud. He was ordered to hand back around $22 billion and sentenced to ten years in prison.

Dennis Kozlowski built Tyco, an obscure New England electronics maker, into one of America's biggest conglomerates through an audacious series of mergers and acquisitions after assuming the role of chief executive in 1992. Mr Kozlowski led an extravagant life but the cash that paid for it was ill-gotten.

"$2m birthday party for Mr Kozlowski's wife"

Mr Kozlowski and Mark Swartz, Tyco's former finance chief, were accused of looting $600m from the firm through fraudulent share sales and unauthorised compensation. Their first court appearance ended in a mistrial after the only juror pressing for acquittal complained that she felt threatened. However, many examples of the misuse of Tyco's money emerged: $2m birthday party for Mr Kozlowski's wife in Sardinia featuring an ice sculpture of Michelangelo's David dispensing vodka; a lavish $18m Manhattan apartment; a $6,000 shower curtain and jewellery, flowers, clothing and wine. After a second trial in June 2005 both men were found guilty and were sentenced to up to 25 years in jail.

Ivar Kreuger, "the Swedish match king", gained monopolies for match production in many countries after the first world war. He then set up the International Match Corporation in America, which went on to control two-thirds of world match production. But his business began to fail after the Wall Street crash of 1929 and he hit a liquidity crisis. He was found dead in a hotel room in Paris in 1932 having seemingly shot himself. After his death, it was discovered that, through false accounting, American investors had been fleeced of millions of dollars.

Nick Leeson worked for Barings, a respectable and long-established bank based in the City of London. His work, trading futures on the Singapore Monetary Exchange, led to big losses when bets on the future direction of the Japanese stockmarket went spectacularly wrong after the Kobe earthquake of 1995 sent Asian markets plummeting. He kept the losses hidden from his superiors and made a series

❝when his losses hit $1.4bn Mr Leeson went on the run❞

of increasingly risky investments in an effort to recoup the cash. These failed, and when his losses hit $1.4 billion Mr Leeson went on the run. He was apprehended in Germany and sent back to Singapore where he was sentenced to six-and-a-half years in prison. Barings collapsed and was bought by ING, a Dutch insurance giant, for the nominal sum of £1.

Robert Maxwell was born Jan Ludwik Hoch in Czechoslovakia in 1923. He fled the Nazis in 1939 and fought with the British during the second world war, calling himself du Maurier, after a brand of classy

bad boys continued

cigarettes. After the war he came to Britain and changed his name to Maxwell. In 1951 he purchased Pergamon Press, publisher of textbooks and scientific journals, and published a lot of material from communist eastern Europe, where he developed good connections. In 1964 he became a Labour member of parliament, but a financial scandal put an end to his political career five years later. However, in 1974 the "bouncing Czech" repurchased Pergamon, over which he had lost control, and during the 1980s he built up a substantial publishing empire, which included Macmillan, a big US publisher, and Britain's Mirror Group Newspapers. As the 1980s progressed, Maxwell's financial machinations began to catch up with him. In 1991 it was reported that Maxwell had disappeared from his luxury motor yacht off the Canary Islands and not long after his body was found floating some distance away. After he was buried on the Mount of Olives overlooking Jerusalem, it emerged that he had looted £400m from the Mirror Group's

❝it emerged that he had looted £400m from the Mirror Group's pension fund❞

pension fund to prop up his other business interests. Did he jump or was he pushed? Some claim that Mossad agents were behind his death. It is more likely, however, that he knew the game was finally up and couldn't face the consequences.

Michael Milken, the "junk bond king" of Wall Street, financed a slew of corporate takeovers in the 1980s through the pioneering use of high-yield high-risk bonds, making vast sums for himself and his employer, Drexel Burnham Lambert, in the process. He and co-conspirators constructed a web of deceitful transactions that led to 98 charges of racketeering, insider trading and securities fraud, and in 1989, he was sentenced to ten years in prison for securities fraud – "the greatest criminal conspiracy the financial world has ever known". In 1991 his sentence was reduced to two years in prison and three years' probation. In 1998 he settled with the government, paying $42m plus interest. Since then Mr Milken has devoted much of his time and money to charity work.

Asil Nadir, the former boss of Polly Peck International, a British-based conglomerate that included an electronics business and the Del Monte fruit business acquired through a series of audacious acquisitions, fled to northern Cyprus to take advantage of its lack of an extradition treaty with Britain (which does not recognise the territory) after the firm collapsed with previously concealed debts of over £1 billion. The businessman, who had made generous donations to Britain's Conservative Party (to its subsequent embarrassment), was facing 66 charges of theft amounting to £34m but fled by private jet in 1993, shortly before he was due to stand trial. He still lives in northern Cyprus with the hope that one day he will be able to cut a deal that will allow him to return to Britain.

Charles Ponzi was born in Italy and moved to America in 1903, taking a series of menial jobs before launching a scheme in 1919 that promised to double investors' money in 90 days. By 1920 he had taken millions of dollars by paying former investors with later deposits, thus requiring ever greater numbers of dupes to join the scam. The business collapsed only after 40,000 people had handed over some $15m. Despite a wrangle over jurisdiction, Ponzi got five years in federal prison for mail fraud and was later sentenced to seven to nine years in Massachusetts. He jumped bail and started up a new scheme in Florida based on selling land. This collapsed and he received another year in jail, and was sent back to Boston to serve his former sentence. Ponzi died in poverty

> **promised to double investors' money in 90 days**

bad boys continued

in Rio de Janeiro in 1949 but his legacy is the pyramid-selling schemes that still bear his name.

Yoshiaki Tsutsumi was briefly adjudged the world's richest man at the height of Japan's property boom in the late 1980s, having inherited a real estate business from his father who was once said to have owned a sixth of all the land in Japan. But in 2005 Mr Tsutsumi, one of Japan's best-known businessmen, was arrested on suspicion of falsifying shareholder information and selling shares based on the false data. He pleaded guilty and was given a suspended jail sentence and a fine of 5m yen (about $42,000).

Robert Vesco got involved with Bernie Cornfeld's IOS (see above) as a "white knight" to save the foundering fund. He was later accused of looting the company of $224m and fled to Costa Rica after making large illegal contributions to Richard Nixon's re-election campaign. He was charged *in absentia* with theft (and drug smuggling, for good measure). In 1996, Mr Vesco was sentenced to 13 years in prison in Cuba on charges of producing and marketing a miracle cancer cure to overseas investors without the communist government's knowledge.

David Wittig made his fortune on Wall Street before returning to the state of his birth, Kansas, in 1995 as an executive of Westar Energy. He swiftly rose to become chief executive of the utility company and set about establishing

ᴌᴌ the Enron of Kansas ᴊᴊ

himself as a leading member of Topeka's social elite by organising lavish charity events and even buying and renovating at great expense the former governor's mansion. However, in 2002 Mr Wittig and Douglas Lake, a senior executive at Westar, resigned amid accusations that they had systematically looted the company for personal gain and used the corporate jet for personal trips. The case, known as the "Enron of Kansas", came to court at the end of 2003 but ended in a mistrial. After another trial in 2004 the two men were found guilty of conspiracy, wire fraud and money laundering. Mr Wittig was sentenced to 18 years in jail; Mr Lake to 15 years. Each was ordered to pay $5m in fines plus over $53m to Westar.

And some thing fishy...

Bre-X Minerals, a small Canadian firm, bought mining rights on the Busang River in the jungles of Borneo in 1993 little suspecting that it would contain the world's biggest ever deposits of gold ore. By 1995 a geologist, whose keen interest in the high life should have raised alarm, said that the site could produce some 30m ounces of gold. The prospective quantities increased, as did the company's share price. By 1997 investors were led to believe that they were sitting on 200m tonnes of gold, around 8% of the

Bre-X's geologist at the site fell from a helicopter under mysterious circumstances

world's supply. Bigger mining firms made takeover offers. The Indonesian government wanted Bre-X to share its fortune with the people of Indonesia (and a mining firm of its choosing). Bre-X had little choice but to agree. Just before contracts were set to be signed, Bre-X's geologist at the site fell from a helicopter under mysterious circumstances. Shortly afterwards an independent survey revealed that the site contained only insignificant amounts of gold. The firm's share price collapsed from a peak of some C$6 billion to around C$600m, leaving a trail of disgruntled investors (bankruptcy followed in 2002). However, police investigation found no grounds for a criminal prosecution.

Leading management thinkers

Warren Bennis

A laid-back, silver-haired professor at the University of Southern California who has been a hugely influential authority on leadership for decades, consulted by many of the world's most famous leaders, including at least four American presidents. Bennis's fundamental tenet is that leaders are made, not born. But they should not merely be the best manager around. Being a manager is very different from being a leader. "Managers do things right. Leaders do the right thing," is probably Bennis's most famous quotation.

Managers, however, can learn to be leaders. "I believe in 'possible selves'," Bennis has written, "the capacity to adapt and change." To become good leaders, however, people first have to develop as individuals. Among other things, that involves learning not to be afraid of being seen to be vulnerable.

❝ leaving staff to be entirely self-motivated did not work very well ❞

Leadership qualities, he maintains, can only emerge from an "integrated self".

Bennis was greatly influenced by Douglas McGregor (see below) and Theory X and Y. In the late 1960s he tried to run the college where he was provost along the lines of Theory Y. But he found in practice that leaving staff to be entirely self-motivated did not work very well. Many people need more structure and direction than McGregor's scheme allowed.

Howard Schultz, the founder and chairman of Starbucks, says that Bennis once told him that in order to become a great leader you have to develop "your ability to leave your own ego at the door, and to recognise the skills and traits that you need in order to build a world-class organisation".

Marvin Bower

For many years the management-consulting business was dominated by one firm. It advised the world's biggest corporations, and indeed the world's biggest countries, about high-level strategy. So outstanding was the firm that it became known simply as "The Firm".

That firm, McKinsey, was the creation of one man. Not James McKinsey, the man whose name hangs over its front door (and who died young of pneumonia in 1938), but Marvin Bower, the most powerful influence on the firm in the 65 years from McKinsey's death to Bower's own, at the age of 99, in 2003.

Bower modelled the consultancy along the lines of a professional law firm. It was driven by a set of values. For example, the clients' interests came before growth in revenue. "If you looked after the client, the profits would look after themselves," Bower wrote in his 1966 book *The Will to Manage*. But he was not afraid to confront clients. One colleague recalls an occasion when Bower "bellowed out, 'The problem with this company, Mr Little, is you.' And there was a deathly silence. It happened to be totally accurate. That was the end of our work with that client, but it didn't bother Marvin."

> **if you looked after the client, the profits would look after themselves**

The Firm's consultants advise top-flight managers, and they have been sometimes criticised for not being around to follow through the consequences of their advice. They have a reputation for arrogance. *The Economist* once wrote of one of them: "He suffers the lack of self-doubt common in former McKinsey consultants." Some of them, such as Tom Peters and Kenichi Ohmae, have gone on to become gurus in their own right.

The Firm itself is organised in an unusual way. It relies heavily on fresh graduates with MBAs or good degrees

leading management thinkers *continued*

from top universities to churn the numbers and do the analysis of its clients' problems. These are fed into the "teams" that are put together for each project. The graduates stay only for as long as they continue to progress up the hierarchy. If they stick for too long at one level they are asked to leave. The Firm's policy is "up or out".

Jim Collins

A former professor at the Stanford Business School who found himself with a publishing sensation when he expanded his Stanford research about what it takes to make companies endure into a book. *Built to Last*, published in 1994, allowed Collins to retire from teaching.

Collins excels at the American method of empirical business research. He gathers masses of data about a group that he wishes to study (in this case, enduringly excellent companies); then he compares it with a

the best students are those who never quite believe their professors

"carefully selected" control group that is not enduringly excellent, and sees what are the statistically significant differences. It is a method that takes time, and Collins says that *Built to Last* took six years of research.

His second book, *Good to Great* (2001), has become the best-selling business book of all time, overtaking the long-standing holder of that title, *In Search of Excellence*.

Written after Collins had left Stanford, it took five years of research by 21 assistants at his own "management laboratory" in Boulder, Colorado, near the mountains that he loves to climb. Although Collins can command the highest fees on the business lecture circuit (over $100,000 a day), he prefers to stay close to Boulder.

In a sense, Collins took Peters and Waterman's concept of excellence, and what it is to be an excellent company, and stretched it over time. What does it take to be an excellent company decade after decade?

On his website Collins talks of a professor he knew who walked into his first class and wrote on the board: "The best students are those who never quite believe their professors." What then are we to make of Professor Collins's findings?

W. Edwards Deming

Deming was a statistician who applied ideas about variance from a little-known American mathematician, Walter Shewhart, to business processes – and with dramatic effect in terms of quality and productivity. The surprising thing was that he did it not in his native America, but in Japan. To this day Japanese industry awards a prestigious annual prize (called the Deming Prize) to companies that have demonstrated exceptional improvements in quality.

After the second world war Deming was sent to Japan to advise on a census there. He ended up advising Japanese businessmen how to inject quality into their manufacturing industry, which at the time had a reputation around the world for producing shoddy goods. His secret was to demonstrate that all business processes are vulnerable to a loss of quality through variation. Reduce the variation; increase the quality. Deming once said: "If I had to reduce my message for management to a few words, I'd say it all had to do with reducing variation."

Deming's method for bringing this about was built on what became known as the quality circle (or, in Japan, the Deming circle). This is a group of workers who seek to improve the processes they are responsible for in four stages – through planning how to do it, implementing the plan, checking the variance from anticipated outcomes, and taking action to correct it. Spreading this system throughout an organisation has come to be known as TQM (Total Quality Management), and has been adopted in America as widely as in Japan.

Peter Drucker

The most enduring guru of them all. From his 1946 book, *Concept of the Corporation*, based on his wartime experience as a consultant with General Motors, to his 2004 article ("What Makes an Effective Executive?") in the prestigious *Harvard Business Review* – which

> **he never failed to throw light on the tasks and difficulties of management**

won that year's McKinsey prize for the best HBR article of the year – Peter Drucker never failed to throw light on the tasks and difficulties of management.

Born in Austria before the first world war, Drucker moved to England in the late 1920s and thence to America in 1937, where he died in 2005. His academic career did not begin until after the second world war. His interests subsequently were eclectic, and he invented a quiver of management theories – "management by objectives"; decentralisation; and "structure follows strategy". He coined the phrase "knowledge worker" in 1969. But his focus was always on the practical – how to make businesses and their managers perform more effectively.

However, Drucker always set this pragmatic task in a much broader context, and therein lay his enduring appeal. Rosabeth Moss Kanter, a Harvard academic, once wrote: "In the Drucker perspective ... quality of life, technological progress and world peace are all the products of good management ... at root, Drucker is a

management Utopian, descended as much from Robert
Owen as Max Weber."

When Jim Collins (see above) was asked what was the best
advice he ever received, he said it came from Drucker at a
time when Collins was thinking of starting a consulting
business rather than pursuing new business ideas.
Drucker told him, "The real discipline comes in saying
'no' to the wrong opportunities."

Henri Fayol

While American manufacturing processes were being
revolutionised by Taylorism (see below), France's were
being overturned by Fayolism, a method devised by an
engineer, Henri Fayol, who rescued a troubled mining
company and turned it into one of France's most
successful businesses. Fayol's theory was in stark contrast
to Taylor's. He looked for general management principles
that could be applied to a wide range of organisations –
business, financial or even government. He separated the
tasks of management into four categories – planning,
organisation, co-ordination and command – and he was
a great believer in the value of specialisation

❝ he was a great believer in the value of specialisation and the unity of command ❞

and of the unity of command: that each employee should
be answerable to only one person.

Fayol remained virtually unknown outside his native
France until a quarter of a century after his death (in
1949) when his most important work *General and
Industrial Management* – first published in French in 1916
– was finally translated into English. He then became
extraordinarily influential as the founding father of what
became known as the Administration School of
Management. As recently as 1993 he was listed in one
poll as the most popular management writer, alongside
Douglas McGregor.

leading management thinkers /continued

Sumantra Ghoshal

A soft-spoken physicist from Calcutta, Ghoshal began his career at Indian Oil and came to management studies with a solid grounding in corporate life. After doctorates at Harvard and MIT, he worked at INSEAD and the London Business School before dying prematurely at the age of 55 in 2004.

Ghoshal's influence far exceeded his written output. He first made his mark in a seminal critique of the widely used matrix form of organisational structure in which managers reported in two directions – along functional lines and along geographic lines.

❝they argued that dual reporting leads to conflict and confusion❞

Written in 1990 with his closest collaborator, Christopher Bartlett, the article argued that this dual reporting leads to "conflict and confusion". In large multinationals, "separated by barriers of distance, language, time and culture, managers found it virtually impossible to clarify the confusion and resolve the conflicts".

Bartlett and Ghoshal said that companies needed to alter their organisational psychology (the shared norms and beliefs) and their physiology (the systems that allow information to flow around the organisation) before they start to redesign their anatomy (the reporting lines). Their work set off a search for new metaphors for organisational structures – borrowing in particular from psychology and biology (eg, corporate DNA; the left brain of the organisation).

Shortly before he died, Ghoshal wrote one of his most contentious papers which caused a considerable stir. In it, he suggested that much of the blame for corporate corruption in the early 2000s could be laid at the feet of business schools and the way they taught the MBA degree – a point of view shared by Mintzberg and Bennis.

Gary Hamel

Hamel is perhaps best known for the idea of core competence, a phrase that has spread far beyond the management lexicon. He propounded the idea in a 1990 paper written with an Indian academic, C.K. Prahalad. "Core competencies," they wrote, "are the collective learning in the organisation, especially how to co-ordinate diverse production skills and integrate multiple streams of technologies" – in short, the things an

❝core competence, a phrase that has spread far beyond the management lexicon ❞

organisation does particularly well. This dovetailed with the phenomenon of outsourcing, which allowed companies to hand over to others the processes and operations (such as IT or book-keeping) that were not "core", thus freeing them to concentrate on those things that they did best.

Hamel took corporate strategy away from the precision of traditional planning. He recommended that companies identify their core competencies and then reinvent themselves around that base of knowledge and skill. He saw strategy as a matter of revolution, of dramatic change. Strategic innovation, he said, will be the source of competitive advantage in the future.

The brightness of Hamel's star dimmed somewhat in the wake of the Enron collapse. Enron was a company that he had held up as an exemplar of his style of strategic innovation. He had also lauded a number of large Japanese companies whose business model stalled badly at the end of the 20th century.

leading management thinkers *continued*

Michael Hammer

Hammer was a professor of computer science at MIT who came up with the biggest business idea of the 1990s, re-engineering, which he defined as "the fundamental rethinking and radical redesign of business processes to achieve dramatic improvements in critical measures of performance".

The idea was first propounded in a 1990 *Harvard Business Review* article entitled "Re-engineering Work: Don't Automate, Obliterate". This was followed by a book, *Re-engineering the Corporation*, written with James Champy, the founder of the CSC Index consulting firm. The book sold several million copies.

Hammer marked a symbolic shift from a time when traditional mechanical engineers dominated management thinking to an era in which electronic engineers with computer skills became as influential. Re-engineering was a sort of Taylorism updated to take account of information technology.

So popular was re-engineering that one survey in the 1990s showed it to have been adopted by almost 80% of *Fortune* 500 companies. It was often blamed for the widespread lay-offs that became a part of almost every company's radical redesign of its processes at that time.

Hammer never managed to repeat his success. He opened his own consultancy business and worked on the idea of "the process enterprise". If you really want to make re-engineering successful, he argued, you need a whole new type of organisation.

Charles Handy

An Irish protestant whose broad interests spread from

religion and philosophy to the organisation of the workplace. His vivid use of metaphor and accessible writing style have made his books extremely popular – with titles like *The Empty Raincoat* and *The Gods of Management* (in which he identified four different management cultures, which he likened to four Greek Gods: Apollo, Athena, Dionysus and Zeus).

Handy began his career as an employee of the Shell oil company, and was sent to work with a drilling operation in the jungles of Borneo. He later vividly described how little relation his life on the job had to the goal he had been given at headquarters: to maximise the company's return on equity. Handy's written work has almost always been a search for ways in which companies can go beyond the pure pursuit of profit. How can they be transformed into communities and soar above being mere properties to be bought and sold?

> **❝ he was responsible for inventing ideas such as the shamrock organisation ❞**

Handy's academic career began when he went to MIT's Sloan School of Management where, among others, he met Warren Bennis (see above) who, he says, has been his "godfather". He then became a professor at the London Business School where he was responsible for inventing ideas such as the shamrock organisation (which, like the plant, has three leaves – management; specialists; and an increasingly flexible labour force) and portfolio working, a lifestyle in which the individual holds a number of different jobs at the same time.

Robert Kaplan

A Harvard professor credited with coming up with two of the most influential management ideas of the late 20th century: activity-based costing (ABC) and the balanced scorecard. The first is an alternative to traditional accounting where overheads (indirect costs) are allocated

leading management thinkers *continued*

in proportion to an activity's direct costs. For businesses whose goods are customised, this is not a very accurate method. ABC attempts to improve on it by allocating indirect costs more accurately. Popular for a while, ABC fell into disrepute when it became clear that it was much simpler in theory than it was in practice.

The concept of the balanced scorecard was developed with David Norton, a consultant. It starts from the idea that with existing business systems what you measure is what you get. If you measure only financial performance, then financial performance is the target people aim for. In the balanced scorecard things are measured from a number of different perspectives, not just the financial one, but also, for example, from the customer's perspective, from the company's own internal perspective, and from the perspective of innovation and improvement. How can a company continue to create value in the future? The idea appealed to managers who felt that traditional measures of performance were unduly focused on shareholders' interests.

"activity-based costing (ABC) and the balanced scorecard"

Nicolo Machiavelli

The author of one of the most famous books on management ever written, Nicolo Machiavelli remains famous five centuries after the publication of *The Prince*, the short volume in which he outlined what a prince must do to survive and prosper, surrounded as he inevitably is by general human malevolence. Dedicated to Lorenzo de Medici – the greatest patron of Renaissance art – the book draws on examples such as Alexander the Great and the German city states, to teach its readers eternal lessons about how to stay in power. To this day, there are corporate leaders who keep a copy of *The Prince* by their bedside.

Machiavelli's tripartite division of leaders' tactics – "Some princes, in order to hold on to their states securely, have disarmed their subjects; some have kept their subject towns divided; and some have fostered animosity against themselves" – first expounded in Florence in the 1520s, has been developed into a modern theory about corporate structure.

For a long time Machiavelli's advice was considered amoral and dishonourably scheming. But in the 1860s Victor Hugo reinstated him. "Machiavelli," he wrote, "is not an evil genius, nor a cowardly writer. He is nothing but the fact … not merely the Italian fact, he is the European fact." Now we can say with confidence: he is the global fact.

Abraham Maslow

Maslow is the most influential anthropologist ever to have worked in industry. He lived among the Blackfoot Indians of Alberta, Canada (where he "found almost the same range of personalities as I find in our society"), before becoming a professor of psychology at Brandeis University near Boston, Massachusetts.

The eldest of the seven children of Russian Jewish immigrants to America, Maslow is best known for developing the concept of the hierarchy of needs, a framework for thinking about human motivation. We have five different kinds of need, he suggested –

physiological ones (hunger, thirst and so on); safety needs (job security, risk avoidance, etc); social needs (parties, meetings, family);

> **“ he is best known for developing the concept of the hierarchy of needs ”**

esteem needs (also called ego needs) such as self-respect, esteem and sense of achievement; and self-actualisation,

leading management thinkers *continued*

described by Maslow as: "A musician must make music, an artist must paint, a poet must write, if he is to be ultimately happy. What a man can be, he must be. This need we may call self-actualisation."

Needs in the earlier categories have to be satisfied before needs in the higher ones can act as motivators. (Although the image of the starving poet is a recurring one, and not only in fiction.) Any single act may satisfy more than one need. We have a drink at a bar because we're thirsty and also because we want to meet friends.

Douglas McGregor

A social psychologist by training, McGregor spent most of his relatively short life (he died in 1964 at the age of 58) as an academic at Harvard and MIT. Yet in 1993 he was listed as the most popular management writer ever, alongside the Frenchman Henri Fayol.

McGregor was the first effective counterweight to the mechanistic thinking of Taylor's scientific management.

❝theory Y assumes that people will exercise self-direction and self-control ❞

His highly influential idea was expounded in his book *The Human Side of Enterprise*, published in 1960. In it he argued that there are two fundamentally different styles of management. One he called Theory X, an authoritarian style which maintains that management "must counteract an inherent human tendency to avoid work". The other, Theory Y, "assumes that people will exercise self-direction and self-control in the achievement of organisational objectives to the degree that they are committed to those objectives". Management's job is to maximise their commitment.

McGregor urged companies to adopt Theory Y. Only it, he believed, could motivate human beings to the highest levels of achievement. His thinking resounds in today's team-based management styles. But McGregor's bifurcated theory has been criticised (by Abraham Maslow, among others) as being tough on the weaker members of society, those who need guidance. Not everyone is sufficiently self-controlled and self-motivated to thrive in a Theory Y environment.

Henry Mintzberg

A consistently contrary Canadian academic who sometimes seems to be undermining the very industry in which he works, Mintzberg first came to fame with a brilliant article in the *Harvard Business Review* in 1975 entitled "The Manager's Job: Folklore and Fact". He studied what a number of managers in different industrial sectors actually did, day in, day out. And he found that "Jumping from topic to topic, he (the manager) thrives on interruptions and more often than not disposes of items in ten minutes or less. Though he may have 50 projects going, all are delegated." A sample of British managers were found to work for more than half an hour without interruption "about once every two days". So much for careful strategic planning.

In *Managers not MBAs*, published in 2004, Mintzberg argued that the MBA, the bread-and-butter course of many business schools, and the *sine qua non* of fast-track management careers, "prepares people to manage nothing". Synthesis, not analysis, he says, "is the very essence of management", and MBA courses teach only analysis. Failed leaders such as Ford's Robert McNamara and Enron's Jeffrey Skilling, who came near the top of their class at Harvard Business School, were star MBA students and brilliant analysts. That was not enough, however, to turn them into great managers or leaders.

leading management thinkers *continued*

Kenichi Ohmae

The only management guru of any stature to have emerged from Japan. Trained as a nuclear physicist at MIT, Ohmae was head of McKinsey's Tokyo office when he published his most famous book, *Triad Power*, in 1985. At a time when multinational firms were busily spreading their operations around the world, he argued that they needed to be strong in all three major economic blocs – Europe, North America and the Pacific Rim, "the Triad" – if they were to compete successfully against others who were strong in those places.

Ohmae was also influential in spreading the idea that the major difference between Japanese firms and their western counterparts is their time frame. Japanese firms look to the longer-term, while western firms, driven by the demands of their stockmarkets, are more focused on short-term profits. He argued that this short-term focus led western companies to pay too little attention to their customers. "In the long run," he wrote, "the corporation that is genuinely interested in its customers is the one that will be interesting to investors."

> **the difference between Japanese firms and their western counterparts is their time frame**

Ohmae's books are full of Japanese examples and they helped familiarise western audiences with Japan's management breakthroughs – for example, the introduction of the just-in-time (JIT) system at Toyota. Ohmae tells how it came about because one worker, Taiichi Ohno, continually asked why the company needed to (expensively) stockpile vast quantities of components for its production line.

Tom Peters

Tom Peters was the co-author of what was, for over 20 years, the best-selling business book of all time. *In Search of Excellence*, written with his fellow McKinsey consultant, Robert Waterman, was first published in 1987 and has sold millions of copies. Part of its success lay in capturing the zeitgeist of the times. Corporate America was feeling overwhelmed by Japan's evident superiority in manufacturing. It needed a reminder that there were still excellent businesses in the United States.

Peters and Waterman identified 43 American companies out of the *Fortune* 500 that had consistently outperformed the average over a 20-year period. They then identified a number of features these companies had in common –

> **a bias for action, sticking to their knitting, and staying close to their customers**

including a bias for action, sticking to their knitting and staying close to their customers.

After the book was published, the two authors went their separate ways. Peters became an energetic speaker on the business circuit, earnings tens of thousands of dollars per performance. The more retiring Waterman set up his own consultancy. They never wrote another book together although each separately wrote several. Peters's 1987 book *Thriving on Chaos* begins with the memorable line: "There are no excellent companies."

The focus of Peters's later work is the management of continuous change in a chaotic world. His books became ever more popular. *Re-imagine*, published in 2003 by Dorling Kindersley, a publisher famous for its artwork, contains lots of sidebars, exclamation marks and pictures of things like frogs leaping.

Michael Porter

Michael Porter redefined the way that businessmen think

leading management thinkers *continued*

about competition. He began by simplifying the notion of competitive advantage and then created a new framework for companies to think about how to achieve it.

Competitive advantage, he wrote, is "a function of either providing comparable buyer value more efficiently than competitors (low cost) or performing activities at comparable cost, but in unique ways that create more buyer value than competitors and, hence, command a premium price (differentiation)".

Porter maintained that there are five forces driving competition in business:

- existing rivalry between firms;
- the threat of a new entrant to a market;
- the threat of substitute products and services;
- the bargaining power of suppliers;
- the bargaining power of buyers.

Like many leading management thinkers, from Frederick Taylor on, Porter trained first as an engineer. But after a doctorate in economics he became a professor at Harvard Business School. Like Tom Peters, he is a skilful presenter who commands high fees on the lecture circuit.

In his book *Competitive Advantage* (1985), Porter introduced the idea of the value chain, which has been highly influential in subsequent strategic thinking. He created a model in which the firm is structured as a chain of value-creating activities. The chain is divided into five main links – inbound logistics, operations, outbound logistics, marketing and sales, and services.

❝the firm is structured as a chain of value-creating activities❞

In his later work Porter looked at ways in which nations

gain competitive advantage over each other, and this led him to focus on the phenomenon of clustering. Nations did well, he maintained, in large part because of the accumulation of specialised skills and industries that, through dynamic competition between them, brought about superior products and processes.

Frederick Winslow Taylor

A true pioneer, Taylor was, in Peter Drucker's words, "the first man in history who did not take work for granted, but looked at it and studied it. His approach to work is still the basic foundation." Taylor trained as an engineer but then worked as a manager at the Midvale Steel Works in Philadelphia. There he took to walking around with a stop-watch and a notepad breaking down manual tasks into a series of components and thereby measuring the workers' productivity. Out of this grew the idea of piece work.

Taylor's first book, *A Piece-Rate System*, was published in 1895. A later publication made him the author of the very first business bestseller, *The Principles of Scientific Management*, published in 1911. Its influence spread to unlikely places. Lenin at one time exhorted Soviet workers to "try out every scientific and progressive suggestion of the Taylor system".

Lenin exhorted workers to 'try out every scientific and progressive suggestion of the Taylor system'

Subsequent failure to achieve Taylor-like production targets led many Soviet workers to the gulag.

Today, scientific management – sometimes called "Taylorism" – is often seen as representing the dehumanising aspect of industrialisation, a system that has no room for the nuances of human nature as it surges on to find the one best way.

Sun Tzu

The ultimate military strategist, Sun Tzu was a general who lived in China over 2,400 years ago whose victories would be no more recalled than those of many other military leaders had he not put down his thoughts in a slim tome (of a mere 25 pages of text). Called in the original Chinese, *The Military Method of Mr Sun*, today the book is better known as *The Art of War*.

The Art of War contains much wisdom of relevance today.

> **why destroy when you can win by stealth and cunning**

For example, Sun Tzu asks: "Why destroy when you can win by stealth and cunning?" His fundamental strategy is a bit like that of judo: undermine your enemy by using the power of his own momentum against him.

Gary Hamel (see above) put Sun Tzu in his proper place when he wrote: "Strategy didn't start with Igor Ansoff, neither did it start with Machiavelli. It probably did not even start with Sun Tzu. Strategy is as old as human conflict." Nevertheless, *The Art of War* is still almost compulsory reading for businessmen in the east. Sun Tzu's advice to businessmen in the west would probably be: "To beat your enemies, first know their strategy – or at least where they are likely to be getting that strategy from."

The oldest stock exchanges

Exchange	City	Founding year
Amsterdam Stock Exchange	Amsterdam	1602
Paris Bourse	Paris	1724
Philadelphia Stock Exchange	Philadelphia	1790
London Stock Exchange	London	1801*
Milan Stock Exchange	Milan	1808
New York Stock Exchange	New York	1817†
Frankfurt Stock Exchange	Frankfurt	1820‡
Bolsa de Madrid	Madrid	1831
Toronto Stock Exchange	Toronto	1861
Australian Stock Exchange	Sydney	1872
Bombay Stock Exchange	Mumbai	1875
Zurich Stock Exchange	Zurich	1877
Tokyo Stock Exchange	Tokyo	1878
Chicago Stock Exchange	Chicago	1882
Pacific Stock Exchange	San Francisco	1882
Johannesburg Stock Exchange	Johannesburg	1887
Bovespa	São Paulo	1890
Hong Kong Stock Exchange	Hong Kong	1891
Cairo Stock Exchange	Cairo	1903
Istanbul Stock Exchange	Istanbul	1929**
Mercado de Valores (Merval)	Buenos Aires	1929
NASDAQ	United States	1971
Stock Exchange of Singapore	Singapore	1973

*Preceded by Jonathan's Coffee House, records beginning 1698.
†Preceded by the Buttonwood Agreement, signed 1792.
‡First share issue traded; had existed as bond exchange since late 18th century.
**Originally Istanbul Securities and Foreign Exchange Bourse.
Note: Amsterdam is not the only exchange claiming to be the oldest but it does seem to have been the first established stock exchange.
Sources: stock exchanges; www.interactivebrokers.com

Leading stockmarkets

Total market capitalisation, 2005, $bn		Total value traded, 2005, $bn	
US	16,998	US	21,510
Japan	4,737	Japan	4,997
UK	3,058	UK	4,167
France	1,710	Germany	1,763
Canada	1,481	Spain	1,557
Germany	1,221	France	1,476
Hong Kong	1,006	South Korea	1,203
Spain	960	Italy	1,115
Switzerland	939	Saudi Arabia	1,104
Australia	804	Switzerland	883
Italy	798	Canada	845
China	781	Netherlands	757
Netherlands	728	Taiwan	618
South Korea	718	Australia	616
Saudi Arabia	646	China	586
South Africa	565	Sweden	464
India	553	Hong Kong	460
Russia	549	India	443
Taiwan	486	Finland	273
Brazil	475	South Africa	201
Sweden	404	Turkey	201
Belgium	327	Norway	195
Mexico	239	Russia	159
UAE	226	Brazil	154
Finland	210	Denmark	152
Singapore	208	UAE	143
Norway	191	Pakistan	141
Malaysia	181	Singapore	120
Denmark	178	Belgium	114
Turkey	162	Kuwait	94
Greece	145	Thailand	89
Chile	136	Greece	65
Kuwait	130	Ireland	65
Austria	126	Israel	60
Thailand	124	Mexico	53
Israel	120	Malaysia	50
Ireland	114	Austria	46
Poland	94	Indonesia	42
Qatar	87	Czech Republic	41
Indonesia	81	Portugal	39

Source: Standard & Poor's

Number of listed domestic companies

End year, '000	1995	2005		1995	2005
US	7.67	5.14	Russia	0.17	0.30
India	5.40	4.76	Italy	0.25	0.28
Canada	1.20	3.72	Switzerland	0.23	0.26
Spain	0.36	3.30	Chile	0.28	0.25
Japan	2.26	3.28	Sweden	0.22	0.25
UK	2.08	2.76	Philippines	0.21	0.24
Australia	1.18	1.64	Slovakia	0.02	0.21
South Korea	0.72	1.62	Peru	0.25	0.20
China	0.32	1.39	Norway	0.15	0.20
Hong Kong	0.52	1.13	Netherlands	0.22	0.17
Malaysia	0.53	1.02	Mexico	0.19	0.15
Egypt	0.75	0.74	Belgium	0.14	0.15
Taiwan	0.35	0.70	New Zealand	0.13	0.15
Pakistan	0.76	0.66	Slovenia	0.02	0.12
France	0.45	0.66	Colombia	0.19	0.11
Germany	0.68	0.65	Argentina	0.15	0.10
Israel	0.65	0.57	Austria	0.11	0.09
Singapore	0.21	0.56	Saudi Arabia	0.07	0.08
Thailand	0.42	0.47	Venezuela	0.09	0.05
South Africa	0.64	0.39	Latvia	0.02	0.05
Brazil	0.54	0.38	Ireland	0.08	0.05
Indonesia	0.24	0.34	Hungary	0.04	0.04
Turkey	0.21	0.30	Lithuania	0.35	0.04

Source: Standard & Poor's

Some stockmarket indices explained

Australia All Ordinaries Index

Australia's All Ordinaries Index comprises nearly 500 companies, representing 95% of Australia's market capitalisation. Constituents are reviewed on an annual basis. Its base value is 500 as of December 31st 1979.

CAC 40 Index

The CAC 40 is France's benchmark index for the Paris Bourse. CAC stands for "*Cotation Assistée en Continu*", or "continuous-time computer-assisted quotation". The index comprises the 40 biggest companies on the Paris Bourse. It has a base value of 1,000 starting on December 31st 1987. The index is reviewed quarterly.

DAX 30 Index

The DAX (*Deutsche Aktienindex*) 30 is composed of Germany's 30 largest and most liquid listed companies. Its base value is 1,000 starting on December 31st 1987. Unlike most stock indices, the DAX includes dividend calculations and thus is a measure of total returns, not just price performance.

Dow Jones Industrial Average Index

The Dow Jones Company started tracking an index of 12 industrial companies' stock prices on May 26th 1896. It now comprises 30 stocks which are no longer necessarily in the industrial sector. The index is price-weighted, rather than market-capitalisation weighted, unlike most major stock indices. Also unlike most other indices, its component companies change irregularly and rarely, and changes are based not on specific criteria but the judgment of editors of the *Wall Street Journal*. It is the most quoted stockmarket index in print, television and internet media.

FTSE Actuaries All-Share Index and FTSE 100 Index

The FTSE ("Footsie") indices derive their name from the acronym for the "Financial Times Stock Exchange" index. The All-Share index was first calculated in 1962. The more closely followed FTSE 100 index began on January 3rd 1984, with a value of 1,000. It includes the top 100 listed firms by market capitalisation on the London Stock Exchange and is reviewed quarterly. The FTSE 250, created in 1985, represents mid-capitalisation companies in Britain not covered by the FTSE 100 and has become increasingly popular in recent years.

Hang Seng Index

The Hang Seng Index derives its name from Hong Kong's Hang Seng Bank, which created the index in 1969. Optimistically, "Hang Seng" means "ever-growing" in Chinese. It comprises the 33 largest companies drawn from four industry groups, and accounts for about 70% of the Hong Kong stockmarket's value. The index's base value is 100, corresponding to August 1964.

IGBM – Madrid General Index

The IGBM (*Índice General de la Bolsa de Madrid*) is the principal index in Spain. It includes almost 90 companies which are reviewed on an annual basis. It has a base date of December 31st 1985 with a value of 100.

MSCI Emerging Markets Free Index

The MSCI Emerging Markets Index measures the stockmarket performance of the most popular emerging markets. It currently tracks the markets of 25 emerging-market countries, including: Argentina, Brazil, Chile,

some stockmarket indices *continued*

China, Colombia, Czech Republic, Egypt, Hungary, India, Indonesia, Israel, Jordan, Malaysia, Mexico, Morocco, Pakistan, Peru, Philippines, Poland, Russia, South Africa, South Korea, Taiwan, Thailand and Turkey. It is commonly quoted in US dollar terms.

NASDAQ 100

NASDAQ is the acronym for the "National Association of Securities Dealers Automated Quotations" system. The NASDAQ 100 tracks the performance of the top 100 companies traded on the NASDAQ exchange system. The NASDAQ is dominated by technology firms, so the performance of the NASDAQ 100 is closely watched as a barometer for the information-technology industry.

Nikkei 225 Index

The Nikkei 225 is Japan's most closely watched stock index, published by the business daily *Neihon Keizai Shimbun* (*Nikkei*). It measures the performance of 225 of the top stocks on the Tokyo Stock Exchange. Established on September 7th 1950, but with a base value of 100 starting on May 16th 1949, it is a price-based index like the Dow Jones Industrial Average. It is reviewed at least once a year but only a maximum of six stocks can be replaced each year.

Standard & Poor's 500 Index

Standard & Poor's, a credit-rating agency and provider of securities research, created the S&P 500 index in 1957. However, its base value of 10 represents the average value of its components from 1941 to 1943. The index is designed to reflect the performance of the largest US companies by market capitalisation, but by virtue of the number of constituents, to a significant degree it reflects the market as a whole. It is reviewed at least once a month.

S&P/TSX Composite Index

The Standard & Poor's/Toronto Stock Exchange
Composite Index is Canada's benchmark index. It
includes nearly 300 of the largest companies listed on the
Toronto exchange, accounting for around 70% of its
market capitalisation. The index was launched on
January 1st 1977 with a base value of 1,000 for 1975. Its
constituents are reviewed on a quarterly basis.

Topix Index

Japan's Topix index is a broader stock index than the
Nikkei 225 and includes the stocks of all large companies
(currently about 1,600) on the Tokyo exchange. It is
weighted by market capitalisation and constituents are
reviewed once a year. Its base value of 100 corresponds to
January 8th 1964.

Stockmarket *performance*

Year end	FTSE All-Share Index	FTSE All-Share % change	FTSE 100 Index	FTSE 100 % change	US S&P 500 Index
1980	292.2	27.2	647.4	27.1	135.8
1981	313.1	7.2	684.3	5.7	122.6
1982	382.2	22.1	834.3	21.9	140.6
1983	470.5	23.1	1,000.0	19.9	164.9
1984	592.9	26.0	1,232.2	23.2	167.2
1985	682.9	15.2	1,412.6	14.6	211.3
1986	835.5	22.3	1,679.0	18.9	242.2
1987	870.2	4.2	1,712.7	2.0	247.1
1988	926.6	6.5	1,793.1	4.7	277.7
1989	1,204.7	30.0	2,422.7	35.1	353.4
1990	1,032.3	-14.3	2,143.5	-11.5	330.2
1991	1,187.7	15.1	2,493.1	16.3	417.1
1992	1,363.8	14.8	2,846.5	14.2	435.7
1993	1,682.2	23.3	3,418.4	20.1	466.5
1994	1,521.4	-9.6	3,065.5	-10.3	459.3
1995	1,803.1	18.5	3,689.3	20.3	615.9
1996	2,013.7	11.7	4,118.5	11.6	740.7
1997	2,411.0	19.7	5,135.5	24.7	970.4
1998	2,673.9	10.9	5,882.6	14.5	1,229.2
1999	3,242.1	21.2	6,930.2	17.8	1,469.3
2000	2,983.8	-8.0	6,222.5	-10.2	1,320.3
2001	2,523.9	-15.4	5,217.4	-16.2	1,148.1
2002	1,893.7	-25.0	3,940.4	-24.5	879.8
2003	2,207.4	16.6	4,476.9	13.6	1,111.9
2004	2,410.8	9.2	4,814.3	7.5	1,211.9
2005	2,847.0	18.1	5,618.8	16.7	1,248.3
1980–2005 %		1,139.0		1,003.4	
1990–2005 %		136.3		131.9	
Starting year:		1980		1980	
Years		26		26	
Compound growth:		8.9		9.7	
Average change:		11.2		10.7	
Standard deviation:		14.5		14.6	

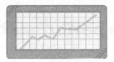

	US				Japan			
S&P 500	Dow Jones		NASDAQ 100		Nikkei 225		Topix	
% change	Index	% change	Index	% change	Index	% change	Index	% change
25.8	964.0	14.9			7,063.1	7.5	491.1	6.9
-9.7	875.0	-9.2			7,681.8	8.8	570.3	16.1
14.8	1,046.5	19.6			8,016.7	4.4	593.7	4.1
17.3	1,258.6	20.3	133.1		9,893.8	23.4	731.8	23.3
1.4	1,211.6	-3.7	108.6	-18.4	11,542.6	16.7	913.4	24.8
26.3	1,546.7	27.7	132.3	21.8	13,083.2	13.3	1,047.1	14.6
14.6	1,896.0	22.6	141.4	6.9	18,820.7	43.9	1,562.6	49.2
2.0	1,938.8	2.3	156.3	10.5	21,564.0	14.6	1,725.8	10.4
12.4	2,168.6	11.8	177.4	13.5	30,159.0	39.9	2,357.0	36.6
27.3	2,753.2	27.0	223.8	26.2	38,915.9	29.0	2,881.4	22.2
-6.6	2,633.7	-4.3	200.5	-10.4	23,848.7	-38.7	1,733.8	-39.8
26.3	3,168.8	20.3	330.9	65.0	22,983.8	-3.6	1,714.7	-1.1
4.5	3,301.1	4.2	360.2	8.9	16,925.0	-26.4	1,307.7	-23.7
7.1	3,754.1	13.7	398.3	10.6	17,417.2	2.9	1,439.3	10.1
-1.5	3,834.4	2.1	404.3	1.5	19,723.1	13.2	1,559.1	8.3
34.1	5,117.1	33.5	576.2	42.5	19,868.2	0.7	1,577.7	1.2
20.3	6,448.3	26.0	821.4	42.5	19,361.4	-2.6	1,470.9	-6.8
31.0	7,908.2	22.6	990.8	20.6	15,258.7	-21.2	1,175.0	-20.1
26.7	9,181.4	16.1	1,836.0	85.3	13,842.2	-9.3	1,087.0	-7.5
19.5	11,497.1	25.2	3,707.8	101.9	18,934.3	36.8	1,722.2	58.4
-10.1	10,786.9	-6.2	2,341.7	-36.8	13,785.7	-27.2	1,283.7	-25.5
-13.0	10,021.5	-7.1	1,577.1	-32.7	10,542.6	-23.5	1,032.1	-19.6
-23.4	8,341.6	-16.8	984.4	-37.6	8,579.0	-18.6	843.3	-18.3
26.4	10,453.9	25.3	1,467.9	49.1	10,676.6	24.5	1,043.7	23.8
9.0	10,783.0	3.1	1,621.1	10.4	11,488.8	7.6	1,149.6	10.2
3.0	10,717.5	-0.6	1,645.2	1.5	16,111.4	40.2	1,649.8	43.5
156.5	1,177.8		na		145.2		258.9	
53.2	289.3		635.0		-58.6		-42.7	
1980	1980		1984		1980		1980	
26	26		22		26		26	
9.9	10.3		12.1		3.5		5.0	
11.0	11.2		17.4		6.0		7.7	
15.5	14.0		36.4		22.8		24.2	

stockmarket *performance* continued

Year end	Hong Kong Hang Seng Index	% change	Canada S&P/TSX Index	% change	Germany DAX 30 Index	% change	France CAC 40 Index
1980	1,473.6	67.6	2,268.7	25.1	480.9	-3.4	
1981	1,405.8	-4.6	1,954.2	-13.9	490.4	2.0	
1982	783.8	-44.2	1,958.1	0.2	552.8	12.7	
1983	874.9	11.6	2,552.3	30.3	774.0	40.0	
1984	1,200.4	37.2	2,400.3	-6.0	820.9	6.1	
1985	1,752.5	46.0	2,900.6	20.8	1,366.2	66.4	
1986	2,568.3	46.6	3,066.2	5.7	1,432.3	4.8	
1987	2,302.8	-10.3	3,160.1	3.1	1,000.0	-30.2	1,000.0
1988	2,687.4	16.7	3,390.0	7.3	1,327.9	32.8	1,573.9
1989	2,836.6	5.5	3,969.8	17.1	1,790.4	34.8	2,001.1
1990	3,024.6	6.6	3,256.8	-18.0	1,398.2	-21.9	1,517.9
1991	4,297.3	42.1	3,512.4	7.8	1,578.0	12.9	1,765.7
1992	5,512.4	28.3	3,350.4	-4.6	1,545.1	-2.1	1,857.8
1993	11,888.4	115.7	4,321.4	29.0	2,266.7	46.7	2,268.2
1994	8,191.0	-31.1	4,213.6	-2.5	2,106.6	-7.1	1,881.2
1995	10,073.4	23.0	4,713.5	11.9	2,253.9	7.0	1,872.0
1996	13,451.5	33.5	5,927.0	25.7	2,888.7	28.2	2,315.7
1997	10,722.8	-20.3	6,699.4	13.0	4,249.7	47.1	2,998.9
1998	10,048.6	-6.3	6,485.9	-3.2	5,002.4	17.7	3,942.7
1999	16,962.1	68.8	8,413.8	29.7	6,958.1	39.1	5,958.3
2000	15,095.5	-11.0	8,933.7	6.2	6,433.6	-7.5	5,926.4
2001	11,397.2	-24.5	7,688.4	-13.9	5,160.1	-19.8	4,624.6
2002	9,321.3	-18.2	6,614.5	-14.0	2,892.6	-43.9	3,063.9
2003	12,575.9	34.9	8,220.9	24.3	3,965.2	37.1	3,557.9
2004	14,230.1	13.2	9,246.7	12.5	4,256.1	7.3	3,821.2
2005	14,876.4	4.5	11,272.3	21.9	5,408.3	27.1	4,715.2
1980–2005		1,591.7		521.7		986.5	
1990–2005		424.5		184.0		202.1	
Starting year:		1980		1980		1980	
Years		26		26		26	
Compound growth:		11.5		7.3		9.6	
Average change:		16.6		8.3		12.8	
Standard deviation:		35.7		14.9		26.4	

Source: Thomson Datastream

France CAC40 % change	Spain Madrid General Index	% change	Australia All Ordinaries Index	% change	Emerging markets MSCI Emg Mkts Free Index	% change
	44.4	6.1				
	55.1	24.0				
	45.1	-18.2				
	52.5	16.5				
	73.9	40.7				
	100.0	35.3				
	208.3	108.3				
	227.2	9.1			100.0	
57.4	274.4	20.8			134.9	34.9
27.1	296.8	8.2			214.7	59.2
-24.1	223.3	-24.8			185.2	-13.8
16.3	246.2	10.3			288.8	56.0
5.2	214.3	-13.0	1,589.1		314.9	9.0
22.1	322.8	50.7	2,153.3	35.5	539.3	71.3
-17.1	285.0	-11.7	1,891.7	-12.1	492.6	-8.7
-0.5	320.1	12.3	2,188.5	15.7	458.4	-6.9
23.7	444.8	39.0	2,404.8	9.9	476.3	3.9
29.5	632.6	42.2	2,579.5	7.3	412.5	-13.4
31.5	867.8	37.2	2,697.0	4.6	299.0	-27.5
51.1	1,008.6	16.2	3,108.8	15.3	489.4	63.7
-0.5	880.7	12.7	3,154.7	1.5	333.8	-31.8
-22.0	824.4	-6.4	3,359.9	6.5	317.4	-4.9
-33.7	634.0	-23.1	2,975.5	-11.4	292.1	-8.0
16.1	808.0	27.4	3,306.0	11.1	442.8	51.6
7.4	959.1	18.7	4,053.1	22.6	542.2	22.4
23.4	1,156.2	20.6	4,708.8	16.2	706.5	30.3
na	2,662.1		na		na	
135.6	289.6		na		229.1	
1988	1980		1993		1988	
18	26		13		18	
9.0	13.6		8.7		11.5	
11.8	16.7		9.4		16.0	
25.1	28.4		12.8		33.4	

$tockmarkets: the best and worst of times

MSCI World Index

Best days				Worst days			
Date	Close	Change, points	Change, %	Date	Close	Change, points	Change, %
21/10/87	418.89	32.47	8.40	19/10/87	421.28	-46.00	-9.84
29/7/02	821.13	39.08	5.00	20/10/87	386.42	-34.87	-8.28
17/1/91	460.54	21.45	4.88	26/10/87	378.35	-24.05	-5.98
15/10/02	786.10	35.37	4.71	19/8/91	472.32	-25.26	-5.08
29/7/02	821.12	35.35	4.50	27/10/97	893.91	-41.34	-4.42
30/10/87	402.28	15.33	3.96	14/4/00	1,329.98	-54.08	-3.91
2/10/90	446.82	16.98	3.95	22/7/02	776.93	-29.21	-3.62
11/10/02	749.32	27.86	3.86	12/3/01	1,093.10	-40.65	-3.59
24/9/01	888.68	32.09	3.75	17/3/80	124.40	-4.60	-3.57
29/9/81	138.60	4.80	3.59	19/7/02	806.14	-29.00	-3.47

MSCI World Index

Best years				Worst years			
Date	Close	Change, points	Change, %	Date	Close	Change, points	Change, %
1933	22.29	9.02	68.02	1931	13.48	-9.40	-41.08
1986	356.83	100.31	39.11	1920	14.98	-6.51	-30.28
1954	38.25	10.60	38.33	1974	78.24	-30.17	-27.83
1985	256.51	69.31	37.02	1930	22.89	-7.63	-25.00
2003	1,036.32	244.10	30.81	1946	22.73	-6.22	-21.47
1958	52.34	12.06	29.95	2002	792.22	-211.30	-21.06
1975	100.86	22.63	28.92	1990	461.53	-105.81	-18.65
1959	66.73	14.39	27.49	2001	1,003.52	-217.73	-17.83
1999	1,420.88	270.93	23.56	1937	24.81	-5.13	-17.13
1998	1,149.95	213.36	22.78	1973	108.41	-22.33	-17.08

US S&P 500 Index

Best days				Worst days			
Date	Close	Change, points	Change, %	Date	Close	Change, points	Change, %
15/3/33	6.81	0.97	16.60	19/10/87	224.84	-57.86	-20.47
30/10/29	22.99	2.56	12.53	28/10/29	22.74	-3.20	-12.34
6/10/31	9.91	1.10	12.43	29/10/29	20.43	-2.31	-10.16
21/9/32	8.51	0.89	11.74	6/11/29	20.61	-2.19	-9.61
5/9/39	12.64	1.11	9.61	18/10/37	10.76	-1.11	-9.34
20/4/33	7.82	0.68	9.52	20/7/33	10.57	-1.03	-8.90
21/10/87	258.38	21.55	9.10	21/7/33	9.65	-0.92	-8.70
14/11/29	19.24	1.58	8.95	26/10/87	227.67	-20.55	-8.28
3/8/32	6.39	0.52	8.80	5/10/32	7.39	-0.66	-8.14
8/10/31	10.62	0.83	8.49	12/8/32	7.00	-0.62	-8.10

US S&P 500 Index

Best years				Worst years			
Date	Close	Change, points	Change, %	Date	Close	Change, points	Change, %
1862	2.63	0.94	55.36	1931	8.12	-7.22	-47.04
1933	10.10	3.21	46.62	1937	10.54	-6.64	-38.64
1954	35.99	11.17	45.03	1907	6.57	-3.27	-33.23
1843	2.33	0.72	45.02	1857	1.48	-0.67	-30.99
1879	4.92	1.48	42.96	1917	6.80	-3.00	-30.61
1935	13.44	3.94	41.51	1854	2.03	-0.88	-30.21
1958	55.21	15.22	38.06	1974	68.56	-28.99	-29.72
1863	3.63	1.00	38.01	1930	15.34	-6.11	-28.48
1928	24.35	6.69	37.88	1920	6.81	-2.21	-24.51
1908	9.03	2.46	37.44	2002	879.82	-268.26	-23.37

Note: These calculations are based on monthly data 1800–1917; weekly data 1918–27; daily data from 1928.

stockmarkets: best and worst _continued_

Financial Times 30 Industrials

Best days				Worst days			
Date	Close	Change, points	Change, %	Date	Close	Change, points	Change, %
23/9/31	56.89	6.46	12.81	20/10/87	951.95	-120.45	-11.23
24/1/75	91.29	7.81	9.36	19/10/87	1,072.40	-117.52	-9.88
10/2/75	117.53	9.31	8.60	1/3/74	138.40	-10.87	-7.28
29/9/38	79.90	6.20	8.41	26/10/87	863.73	-66.60	-7.16
30/1/75	106.22	7.13	7.20	29/5/62	261.30	-18.00	-6.44
7/2/75	108.22	6.36	6.24	2/1/75	62.60	-4.29	-6.41
30/3/71	352.20	20.50	6.18	31/1/75	236.90	-15.40	-6.10
27/1/75	96.88	5.59	6.12	17/3/75	291.70	-17.80	-5.75
13/3/03	3,486.90	199.86	6.08	8/11/76	291.00	-17.70	-5.73
9/10/59	284.70	16.10	5.99	11/9/01	4,745.98	-287.70	-5.72

Financial Times All-Share Index

Best years				Worst years			
Date	Close	Change, points	Change, %	Date	Close	Change, points	Change, %
1975	158.08	91.19	136.33	1974	66.89	-82.87	-55.34
1824	45.53	21.65	90.67	1721	20.42	-10.11	-33.12
1959	106.93	32.36	43.39	1973	149.76	-68.42	-31.36
1971	193.39	57.13	41.93	2002	1,893.73	-630.15	-24.97
1977	214.53	62.57	41.18	1705	13.51	-4.20	-23.72
1968	168.60	46.42	37.99	1931	21.83	-6.69	-23.46
1954	62.66	16.07	34.48	1825	35.17	-10.35	-22.74
1958	74.57	18.59	33.20	1866	20.89	-6.04	-22.42
1817	19.13	4.71	32.62	1803	16.60	-4.66	-21.92
1967	122.18	29.70	32.12	1694	16.63	-4.34	-20.70

Japan Topix Price Index

Best days				Worst days			
Date	Close	Change, points	Change, %	Date	Close	Change, points	Change, %
2/10/90	1,668.83	145.40	9.54	20/10/87	1,793.90	-307.27	-14.62
21/10/87	1,962.41	168.51	9.39	5/3/53	32.32	-3.10	-8.75
21/8/92	1,251.70	87.93	7.56	30/4/70	159.33	-12.86	-7.47
10/4/92	1,282.56	86.37	7.22	2/4/90	2,069.33	-158.15	-7.10
17/11/97	1,257.85	80.33	6.82	12/9/01	990.80	-67.32	-6.36
31/1/94	1,629.22	101.40	6.64	17/4/00	1,552.46	-101.24	-6.12
6/1/88	1,820.03	112.14	6.57	30/3/53	30.31	-1.93	-5.99
16/4/53	32.79	1.97	6.39	16/8/71	196.99	-12.01	-5.75
21/3/01	1,275.41	75.80	6.32	23/8/90	1,829.25	-110.58	-5.70
6/3/53	34.06	1.74	5.38	10/5/04	1,085.54	-65.35	-5.68

Japan Topix Price Index

Best years				Worst years			
Date	Close	Change, points	Change, %	Date	Close	Change, points	Change, %
1952	32.20	17.46	118.38	1920	2.44	-2.33	-48.83
1972	401.70	202.25	101.40	1990	1,733.83	-1,147.54	-39.83
1932	2.69	1.25	86.31	1946	2.55	-1.05	-29.13
1948	6.47	2.98	85.28	2000	1,203.67	438.53	-25.46
1951	14.75	5.70	62.95	1992	1,307.66	-407.02	-23.74
1999	1,722.20	635.21	58.44	1973	306.44	-95.26	-23.71
1915	2.85	0.98	52.01	1930	1.49	-0.40	-21.09
1949	9.76	3.29	50.89	1997	1,175.03	-295.91	-20.12
1986	1,556.37	506.97	48.31	2001	1,032.14	-251.53	-19.59
2005	1,649.76	500.13	43.50	2002	843.29	-188.85	-18.30

Sources: Global Financial Data (www.globalfinancialdata.com); *The Economist*

Clocking the stockmarkets

When the market opens in:	Local opening times	New York	São Paulo	London	Frankfurt
DST factor:January GMT +/--5		-2	+0	+1	
			the time in		
			São Paulo is		
New York	9:30	9:30	12:30	14:30	15:30
São Paulo	11:00	8:00	11:00	13:00	14:00
London	8:00	3:00	6:00	8:00	9:00
Frankfurt	9:00	8:00	6:00	8:00	9:00
Bombay	10:00	14:30	2:30	4:30	5:30
Singapore	9:00	18:00	21:00	1:00	2:00
Hong Kong	10:00	17:00	20:00	2:00	3:00
Tokyo	9:00	19:00	22:00	0:00	1:00
Sydney	10:00	18:00	21:00	23:00	0:00

Sources: Stock exchanges; *The Economist* diary

+5.5	+8	+8	+9	+11
		the time in		
Bombay	Singapore	Hong Kong	Tokyo	Sydney
		is		
20:00	22:30	22:30	23:30	1:30
18:30	21:00	21:00	22:00	0:00
13:30	16:00	16.00	17:00	19:00
13:30	16:00	16.00	17:00	19:00
10:00	12:30	12:30	13:30	15:30
6:30	9:00	9:00	10:00	12:00
7:30	10:00	10:00	11:00	13:00
5:30	8:00	8:00	9:00	11:00
4:30	7:00	7:00	8:00	10:00

Investment [formulas]/²

Black-Scholes model

A pricing model for options that ranks among the most
influential. It was devised by Fischer Black and Myron
Scholes, two Chicago academics, in 1973, the year that
formalised options trading began on the Chicago Board of
Trade. Behind the model is the assumption that asset
prices must adjust to prevent arbitrage between various
combinations of options and cash on the one hand and
the actual asset on the other.

Call price = $S[N(d_1)] \angle E/e^{rt}[N(d_2)]$

Where:

S = current stock price
$N(d_1)$ = normal distribution function of d_1
E = exercise price of option
e = the base of natural logarithms (= 2.718)
r = risk-free interest at an annual rate
t = time to expiry of option (as a fraction of a year)
$N(d_2)$ = normal distribution function of d_2

To solve for d_1:
$d_1 = [\ln(S/E) + (r + 0.5sd^2)t] / [sd(t)^{1/2}]$
Where:
$\ln(S/E)$ = the natural log of S/E
sd = the standard deviation of annual returns on the share price
(where the share price is squared, it is the variance)

To solve for d_2:
$d_2 = d_1 {}_- [sd(t)^{1/2}]$

Capital asset pricing model

Because of its comparative simplicity, the capital asset
pricing model (CAP-M) is a much-used formula for
modelling the theoretically correct price of assets and
portfolios.

$E(R_s) = RF + \beta_s[E(R_m) \angle RF]$

Where:

$E(R_s)$ = the expected return on security $_s$
RF = the risk-free rate of return
β_s = the beta of security $_s$
$E(R_m)$ = the expected return on the market

Capital fulcrum point

An important formula for valuing a warrant, which measures the minimum annual percentage increase required from the value of the underlying ordinary shares for investors to hold warrants in a company's shares in preference to the shares themselves.

$$CFP = [(e/(s-w))^{1/y}] \times 100\%$$
Where:
e = exercise price   s = share price
w = warrant price   y = years to expiry of warrant

Capital market line

The graphical depiction of the trade-off between risk and return for an efficient portfolio. In other words, it is a chart line which shows how much extra return investors would expect for taking on extra risk.

$$[E(R_m) \angle RF]/[sd(R_m)]$$
defines the slope of the market line, where:
$E(R_m)$ = the expected return from the market
RF = the risk-free rate of return
$sd(R_m)$ = the standard deviation of returns from the market

Thus the expected return from any portfolio on the capital market line is:

$$E(R_p) = RF + \{[E(R_m) \angle RF]/[sd(R_m)]\}sd(R_p)$$

Where:
$E(R_p)$ = the expected return on portfolio $_p$
$sd(R_p)$ = the standard deviation of returns on portfolio $_p$

Dividend discount model

A tool for valuing a stock or share which says that the value of the share equals the present value of all its future dividends. It provides a basis for comparing the price of

investment [formulas]/^{2} *continued*

shares in the market with their theoretical value and thus judging whether the shares are cheap or expensive.

Where the growth rate in dividends is assumed to be constant, the fair price of a common stock can be stated as follows:

$P = D/(k - g)$
Where:
P = the price of the stock
D = expected dividend
k = the required rate of return
g = the expected growth rate in dividends

From this, the required rate of return can stated as:
$k = (D/P) + g$

and the stock's price/earnings ratio as:

$P/E = (D/E) / (k - g)$
Where:
E = the expected level of earnings

Single index model

Shows a security's return as a function of the market's return.

$R_{st} = a_s + b_s(R_{mt}) + e_{st}$
Where:
R_{st} = the return on security $_s$ over period $_t$
a_s = the constant return on security $_s$
b_s = the sensitivity of the security's return to the market's return (ie, its beta)
R_{mt} = the market's return over period $_t$
e_{st} = the difference between the actual return on security $_s$ during a given period $_t$ and its expected return

Source: *Essential Investment*, Philip Ryland, The Economist/Profile Books

Private equity

United States

The United States accounted for 45% of the private-equity funds raised throughout the world in 2005, slightly more than in Europe. Over $100 billion in new private-equity funds was raised (a quarter of which was for venture capital), and almost $140 billion in investments were made. US long-term returns to private equity neared 15% at the end of 2005.

Europe

In 2005, over €59 billion in private-equity funds were raised throughout Europe, more than twice that raised in 2004. This was the first time fundraising exceeded the previous peak of €48 billion in 2000. Around 20% of these funds are expected to be used for venture-capital investments, with most of the rest going towards buy-outs. Over €38 billion was invested in private equity in 2005, which marked the fifth consecutive rise and for the second year running surpassed the previous peak in 2000 of just under €35 billion. Since 1980 to end 2004, European private equity has earned an average 9.5% return on investment.

Britain

Britain accounts for half of the European private-equity market and its national market is second only to the United States. In 2005, £27.3 billion in funds was raised by British private-equity firms, more than half of which was for investments in Britain. Nine-tenths of this was expected to go towards buy-outs rather than venture capital. Since 1980, British private-equity funds have averaged a 14.4% return on investment.

Sources: National Venture Capital Association; European Private Equity & Venture Capital Association; British Venture Capital Association; Thomson Venture Economics

Hedge funds

	Hedge-fund assets, $bn	Number of hedge funds
1990	38.91	610
1991	58.37	821
1992	95.72	1,105
1993	167.79	1,514
1994	167.36	1,945
1995	185.75	2,383
1996	256.72	2,781
1997	367.56	2,990
1998	374.77	3,325
1999	456.43	3,617
2000	490.58	3,873
2001	539.06	4,454
2002	625.55	5,379
2003	820.01	6,297
2004	972.61	7,436
2005	1,105.39	8,661
2006*	1,181.70	8,825

*Q1
Source: Hedge Fund Research

Hedge-fund strategies

Arbitrage: funds that attempt to profit from pricing inefficiencies of the market. This can be done using convertible bonds, fixed-income securities, the shares of companies involved in a merger or acquisition, or any financial instrument where relative values can be exploited by arbitrage. Quantitative funds use sophisticated mathematical models to spot price discrepancies.

Distressed securities: funds that invest in, or sell short, the debt or equity of companies in financial distress, such as bankruptcy or corporate restructuring.

Emerging markets: funds that invest in companies or the sovereign debt of developing countries. Many funds tend to have a regional focus.

Equity hedge: funds that use a mixture of long and short positions. Some try to hedge market risks by limiting market exposure, while more aggressive funds use leverage to magnify potential rewards.

Event-driven: funds that invest in opportunities created by corporate events, such as spin-offs, mergers, bankruptcy, recapitalisation and share buybacks.

Fixed-income: funds that invest in fixed-income instruments. Strategies vary and these funds can specialise in fixed-income arbitrage, convertible bonds, high-yield bonds or mortgage-backed securities.

Macro: funds that make leveraged bets on anticipated price movements of stockmarkets, interest rates, currencies and commodities.

Sector: funds that focus on a particular sector for investment. Popular sectors include energy, financial firms, healthcare and biotechnology, metals and mining, real estate and technology.

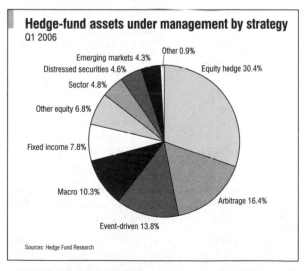

Hedge-fund assets under management by strategy
Q1 2006

Other 0.9%
Emerging markets 4.3%
Distressed securities 4.6%
Sector 4.8%
Other equity 6.8%
Fixed income 7.8%
Macro 10.3%
Event-driven 13.8%
Arbitrage 16.4%
Equity hedge 30.4%

Sources: Hedge Fund Research

Sources: Hedge Fund Research; *The Economist*

Bonds

Credit ratings

	Moody's	Standard & Poor's
Highest credit quality; issuer has strong ability to meet obligations	Aaa	AAA
Very high credit quality; low risk of default	Aa1, Aa2, Aa3	AA+, AA, AA-
High credit quality, but more vulnerable to changes in economy or business	A1, A2, A3	A+, A, A-
Adequate credit quality for now but more likely to be impaired if conditions worsen	Baa1, Baa2, Baa3	BBB+, BBB, BBB-
Below investment grade, but good chance that issuer can meet commitments	Ba1, Ba2, Ba3	BB+, BB, BB-
Significant credit risk, but issuer is currently able to meet obligations	B1, B2, B3	B+, B, B-
High default risk	Caa1, Caa2, Caa3	CCC+, CCC, CCC-
Issuer failed to meet scheduled interest or principal payments	C	D

Source: *Guide to Financial Markets* by Marc Levinson, The Economist/Profile Books

US corporate bonds issued, $bn

	High yield	Investment grade	Total
1990	12.0	152.2	164.2
1991	13.4	210.8	224.2
1992	42.4	250.2	292.6
1993	73.6	329.2	402.8
1994	45.7	260.3	306.0
1995	45.0	285.8	330.8
1996	72.3	336.6	408.9
1997	132.4	423.9	556.3
1998	144.8	563.8	708.6
1999	97.2	657.2	754.4
2000	38.9	703.3	742.2
2001	84.6	792.3	876.9
2002	57.5	593.9	651.4
2003	122.8	640.9	763.7
2004	109.3	619.6	728.9
2005	74.8	632.7	707.5

Note: High-yield bonds are below investment grade so likely to be more speculative and volatile.
Sources: Thomson Financial Securities Data; Bond Market Association

International bond and note issues

	2005, $bn	Stocks, end March 2006
Floating rate issues	1,465	4,264
Straight fixed-rate issues	2,332	10,186
Equity-related issues	43	328
US dollar	1,318	na
Euro	1,838	na
Yen	115	na
Other currencies	569	na
Developed countries	3,454	13,154
United States	837	3,602
Euro area	1,797	6,528
Japan	54	273
Offshore centres	50	179
Emerging markets	230	903
Financial institutions	3,177	11,135
Private	2,749	9,503
Public	428	1,633
Corporate issuers	234	1,587
Private	203	1,355
Public	30	233
Governments	323	1,514
International organisations	106	542
Total announced issues, gross	3,839	14,778

Source: Bank for International Settlements

Bubbles that burst

Tulipmania

Tulips were introduced into western Europe from Turkey in the 16th century. In the 17th century they gave rise to one of the most curious episodes in Holland's history. In the early 1600s single-colour tulips were being sold at relatively modest prices in Dutch markets, but as new varieties were created the fashion for tulips intensified and prices soared. By 1623 a particularly admired and rare variety, *Semper Augustus*, was selling for 1,000 florins for a single bulb, more than six times the average annual wage. Ten years later the price had increased more than fivefold, and then reached a peak at the height of the tulip craze of some 10,000 florins, roughly the same as it cost to buy a fine canalside house in the centre of Amsterdam.

As the mania took hold more and more people sought to cash in on the boom, and the tulip business developed from dealing in actual bulbs to dealing in what were in effect tulip futures.

It couldn't last, and it didn't. In 1637 the bulb bubble burst when it became clear that at the end of the long chain of those speculating in bulb futures there was no one who actually wanted to buy the bulbs at such high prices. Within a period of a few months the market had crashed leaving thousands of people ruined.

The Mississippi Bubble

In 1716 John Law, a Scottish businessman who had come to France two years earlier, persuaded the French government, which was in financial distress, to let him set up a bank that could issue bank notes, which he believed would provide a spur to commerce and help get the government out of its financial difficulties. At the time France controlled the Louisiana colony, which covered an area larger than France itself. In August 1717 Law bought a controlling interest in the then derelict Mississippi Company and was granted a 25-year monopoly by the French government on trade with the West Indies and North America. The company acquired other French trading companies and was renamed the Compagnie des Indes, in effect controlling all French trade outside Europe. Law had raised money to fund the Mississippi Company's activities by issuing shares that could be purchased using notes issued by Law's Banque de Generale or government bonds.

As Law's business empire grew and there was more and more excitement about the riches that were to be exploited across the Atlantic, the share price rose dramatically. People from outside France as well as within couldn't get enough of the shares and Law issued more and more banknotes to enable people to buy them. By the end of 1819, the year of initial issue, the share price had increased twentyfold.

The crunch came at the beginning of 1820 when investors started to sell shares and realise their gains in gold. Law stepped in to prevent people being paid more than a certain amount in gold for their shares, with the rest being payable in notes. Within a year the share price had fallen to a tenth of its value at the peak and Banque de Generale notes were worth only half their face value. A year later the shares were back to their issue price, and Law subsequently took his leave of France. Opinion is divided as to whether Law was in fact a rogue or simply an honest man undone by a misguided scheme.

The South Sea Bubble

In 1711 the South Sea Company was given a monopoly of all trade to the South Seas in return for assuming a

bubbles that burst continued

portion of the national debt that England had accumulated during the War of the Spanish Succession, which had started in 1703 and was still continuing. It was anticipated that when the war ended, which it did in 1713, there would be rich trade pickings to be had among the Spanish colonies in South America. But the South Sea Company did little trading, preferring to accumulate money from investors attracted by its future prospects.

War between Spain and England broke out again in 1718 and the following year the South Sea Company made a proposal to assume the whole of England's national debt. Inducements were offered to influential people and the proposal was accepted. New shares were issued in the company and the stock price was talked up and up.

Speculation fever took hold; a large number of companies that were to trade in the "New World" or which had other supposedly promising futures were set up, many of which were plain and simple scams to separate investors from their money. Confidence in the market was dented and in an effort encouraged by the managers of the South Sea Company to restore it, the "Bubble Act" was passed in 1720 requiring all joint stock companies to have a royal charter. It did the trick: the South Sea Company's share price increased more than fivefold in four months to reach over £1,000. And then the bubble burst – or rather started to deflate. A gradual slide in the share price accelerated and within three months the company was worthless. Many people were ruined and a committee set up in 1721 to investigate the affair discovered widespread corruption involving businessmen and politicians.

Railway mania

The British "railway mania" of the 1840s and the American railway boom up to 1873 shared many similarities. Rail entrepreneurs used the stockmarket to raise huge sums to build proposed lines. Overinvestment led to excess capacity, failing revenues and defaults on loans – so much capital was diverted to railway projects that other businesses suffered and interest rates spiralled. In America, generous land grants helped railroad construction and around 170m acres was given to some 80 rail companies, though half the projected lines were never built. The railway bubble burst in the "Panic of 1873", the same year as America's first successful train robbery.

The Wall Street crash

In 1929 stock prices were 400% higher than they had been in 1924, pushed up way beyond any relationship with the actual worth of their companies, as investors, lured by the prospect of easy riches, piled into the market, accumulating some $6 billion of debt in the process. In early September 1929 prices fell sharply but recovered before falling again. In late October panic selling gave rise to the Wall Street crash, which ushered in a worldwide economic crisis, the Great Depression. Many shareholders were ruined, banks and businesses failed, and unemployment subsequently rose to around 17m.

Japan's monetary mistake

When through the Plaza Accord in 1985 Japan agreed to loosen its monetary policy to boost the value of the yen and trim its exports, things did not turn out quite as expected. Rather than restraining Japanese companies, the sudden doubling of the value of the yen against other currencies allowed big multinational firms to go on a buying spree of American and European assets, using bank loans and the rising value of their property portfolios as collateral. Bank lending on property ballooned as the initial loans drove up land prices and the higher land prices made those loans look like good business. At the height of the boom, the property around the imperial palace in Tokyo was worth more than California, and Australia paid off its national debt by selling a small parcel

bubbles that burst *continued*

of land around its embassy. When the bubble burst after rises in interest rates in the early 1990s, property values slumped. Japan's banks and corporations have since struggled under the weight of bad debts and the country has endured years of economic stagnation that are partly attributable to the bubble and its bursting.

The dotcom boom and bust

The late 1990s saw a speculative frenzy of investment in internet-related shares as investors took the view that anything that would take advantage of the burgeoning popularity of the new technology was certain to make buckets of money. Venture capitalists threw money at any half-baked scheme as long as the entrepreneurs projected vast profits in a short space of time. Huge sums were spent on notional projects to build market share and vast increases in share price accompanied initial public offerings of the firms that were taken to market, making dotcom millionaires overnight (on paper at least). The dotcom boom rubbed off on other shares, especially technology stocks of any kind. Investors poured money into the stockmarket seeking to benefit from its seemingly inexorable rise.

In 1999 stockmarkets around the world hit record peaks. The January 2000 Super Bowl featured 17 dotcom companies which had each paid over $2m for a 30-second spot. But not long after, share prices for e-businesses started to fall as it finally struck home that firms were burning through cash with no prospect of ever making a profit. Eventually, all but the most robust dotcoms went to the wall and stockmarkets plunged, with Nasdaq falling by over 70% between 1999 and 2002. In addition to the heavy losses incurred by institutional investors, millions of private investors lost substantial amounts of money, not to mention their confidence in the stockmarket.

Oil reserves and prices

Proven reserves, barrels, bn

	North America	South & Central America	Europe & Eurasia	Middle East	Africa	Asia Pacific
end 1985	101.5	62.9	78.6	431.3	57.0	39.1
end 1995	89.0	83.8	81.5	661.5	72.0	39.2
end 2005	59.5	103.5	140.5	742.7	114.3	40.2

Source: BP

Average oil price*

	$ per barrel		$ per barrel
1946	1.4	1987	19.2
1950	2.6	1988	16.0
1960	3.0	1989	19.6
1970	3.4	1990	24.5
1971	3.6	1991	21.6
1972	3.6	1992	20.6
1973	3.9	1993	18.4
1974	10.4	1994	17.2
1975	11.2	1995	18.4
1976	12.6	1996	22.0
1977	14.3	1997	20.6
1978	14.9	1998	14.4
1979	22.4	1999	19.3
1980	37.4	2000	30.3
1981	36.7	2001	25.9
1982	33.6	2002	26.1
1983	30.4	2003	31.0
1984	29.4	2004	41.4
1985	28.0	2005	56.8
1986	15.1	2006†	67.4

* West Texas Intermediate (WTI).

†Jan–Jun average.

Sources: Dow Jones Energy Service; Thomson Datastream

Gold reserves and prices

	m ounces, year-end	Gold bullion av. price per troy oz, $
1970	1,059.74	35.65
1971	1,030.28	40.79
1972	1,021.52	58.24
1973	1,024.09	98.01
1974	1,022.08	158.25
1975	1,019.87	161.98
1976	1,015.38	125.09
1977	1,030.35	148.00
1978	1,037.98	193.46
1979	946.89	307.37
1980	955.52	612.24
1981	955.15	459.79
1982	951.23	376.19
1983	950.11	423.45
1984	948.98	360.57
1985	951.45	317.64
1986	951.44	367.82
1987	954.94	446.75
1988	946.65	437.03
1989	940.93	381.52
1990	938.90	383.70
1991	937.80	362.39
1992	928.86	343.83
1993	919.72	360.11
1994	915.67	384.27
1995	907.21	384.29
1996	905.38	387.77
1997	888.56	331.19
1998	968.41	294.23
1999	967.07	278.85
2000	952.09	279.15
2001	942.76	271.16
2002	931.18	310.37
2003	913.56	364.00
2004	900.84	409.79
2005	882.02	445.31
2006	879.84*	594.21†

*Jan–Apr average. †Jan–Jun average.

Note: It was in 1971 that the dollar was finally cut loose from the gold standard, signalling the end of the Bretton Woods arrangements.

Sources: IMF: International Financial Statistics; Thomson Datastream

Gold facts

Gold is a yellow metal. Its chemical symbol is Au from the Latin word *aurum*, which means "glowing dawn".

Gold's atomic number is 79. Its specific gravity, a measure of density, is 19.3-times that of water and it is rated at about 2.5 on Moh's scale of hardness, placing it between gypsum and calcite.

Gold's proportion in an alloy is measured in karats. Pure gold is 24 karats, or 99.999% pure. 100% pure gold is almost impossible to refine.

Gold is the most non-reactive of all metals. It does not react with oxygen and does not rust or tarnish.

Gold will only dissolve in acids such as aqua regia (a mixture of hydrochloric and nitric acids) and some others.

Gold is among the most electrically conductive of all metals. It can convey a tiny electrical current in temperatures between –55°C and 200°C.

Gold is the most ductile of all metals, allowing it to be drawn out into tiny wires or threads without breaking. A single ounce of gold can be drawn into a wire 5 miles long.

Gold's malleability is also unequalled. It can be shaped or extended into very thin sheets. One ounce of gold can be hammered into a 100-sq ft (9.3 sq m) sheet.

Total world production of gold down the ages is estimated at 3 billion ounces (85,000 tonnes). This would fit into a cube with sides measuring 55 feet (16.8m).

Source: The Gold Institute

Rich producers

Silver producers, 2004, tonnes		Gold producers, 2004, tonnes	
Peru	3,060	South Africa	340.4
Mexico	2,531	Australia	259.0
Australia	2,183	US	258.0
China	2,000	China	194.4
Chile	1,360	Russia	180.5
Canada	1,338	Peru	173.2
Poland	1,330	Indonesia	164.4
US	1,246	Canada	130.7
Kazakhstan	690	Uzbekistan	86.0
Bolivia	413	Papua New Guinea	73.5

Platinum producers, 2004, tonnes		Palladium producers, 2004, tonnes	
South Africa	154.6	Russia	127.5
Russia	26.4	South Africa	78.1
North America	10.6	North America	32.2

Diamond producers, 2004, m carats

	Gemstones		Industrial
Russia	21.4	Congo-Kinshasa	22.0
Botswana	23.3	Russia	14.2
Congo-Kinshasa	6.0	Australia	11.3
Australia	9.3	South Africa	8.7
South Africa	5.8	Botswana	7.8
Canada	12.6		
Angola	5.4		
Namibia	2.0		

Sources: World Bureau of Metal Statistics; Johnson Matthey; US Geological Survey

Diamond **and** platinum **facts**

Diamonds Unlike precious metals, top diamond producers by volume are not the same countries as top diamond producers by value. Size and quality vary greatly. One carat = 0.2 grams.

The largest cut diamond is the Golden Jubilee, a yellow diamond weighing 545 carats now part of Thailand's crown jewels. The largest rough diamond is the Cullinan, weighing 3,107 carats and cut into two polished stones, the Great Star of Africa at 530 carats (the second largest polished diamond, now in the Tower of London) and the Lesser Star of Africa at 317 carats, and a further 104 stones.

The highest price paid at auction is the Star of the Season bought in 1995 for $16.5m. It is 100 carats. The diamond bought by Richard Burton for Elizabeth Taylor was 69 carats.

In 2003 thieves broke into the Diamond Centre in Antwerp and stole $100m worth of diamonds from safe-deposit boxes belonging to dealers and cutters.

A diamond was found in 2004 floating in space, the core of a dead star, weighing 10 billion trillion trillion carats, 2,500 miles across, bigger than the moon. It is 50 light years away.

Platinum Platinum is generally 95% pure so does not tarnish or fade, and it is hypoallergenic. As well as being used for jewellery it has industrial and medical uses – catalytic converters and pacemakers.

Behind the currency name

Baht Until the 1940s the Thai currency was known as the tical. A *baht* was a unit of weight of around 15g, the equivalent in silver of one tical.

Bolivar Venezuela's currency takes its name from Simon Bolivar, a Venezulean known as "El Libertador" who led the defeat of Spanish colonialism in the 19th century, gaining independence for his own country as well as Bolivia, Colombia, Ecuador, Panama and Peru. Ecuador's sucre is named after Antonio José de Sucre, also an independence leader and one of Bolivar's closest friends.

Crown The French gold "*denier à la couronne*" was issued by Philip of Valois in about 1339 and featured a large embossed crown. The name was adopted by a slew of countries including the Czech Republic (koruna), Denmark (krone), Estonia (kroon), Iceland (króna), Norway (krone), Sweden (krona).

Dinar Its origin dates back to the most widely used Roman coin, the denarius. The silver coin's name means "containing ten" as it originally equalled ten copper *as*. It survives as the denar in Macedonia and dinar in Algeria, Bahrain, Iraq, Jordan, Kuwait, Tunisia and Serbia

Dollar The name is derived from that of the historic currencies of Bohemia, the tolar, and Germany's thaler. The name *thaler* (from the German *thal*, meaning "valley") itself derives from the *guldengroschen* or "great gulden", a silver coin equal in value to a gold gulden and minted from the silver mined at Joachimsthal in Bohemia. The word "dollar" was in use in English for the thaler for about 200 years before America adopted the term. Spanish dollars, or "pieces of eight", were in circulation in Spain's colonies in the Americas in the 18th century. This and the Maria Theresa Thaler were both in wide use before the American revolution and lent their name to the country's new currency.

Drachma The Greek currency (now superseded by the euro) took its name currency from the verb "to grasp." The Arabic dirham's name is also derived from the ancient drachma.

Dram The Armenian word for "money".

Escudo Taken from the Portuguese (and Spanish) for "shield" and originally Spanish coins decorated with the coat of arms of the king of Spain – the great shield of the house of Hapsburg. The doubloon was a coin originally worth two escudos.

Franc The name is said to derive from the Latin inscription *francorum rex* ("King of the Franks") inscribed on gold coins first made during the reign of Jean le Bon (1350–64).

Guilder The name is taken from coins struck in Florence in the 13th century decorated with a lily, the *florensus*, derived from *fiorino*, Old Italian for flower. The Netherlands adopted the name *gulden*, short for *gulden florijn* (or golden florenus), of which guilder is a corruption. The abbreviation fl or f remained in use. The currency survives in Aruba and the Netherlands Antilles.

Kina Papua New Guinea's money takes its name from the kina shell, which was traditionally used as currency on the island.

Kuna The word means "marten" in Croatian, and is etymologically unrelated to the various currency names derived from the crown. It comes from the use of marten pelts as a trading commodity by medieval merchants.

Kwacha Zambia's currency is taken from the county's main language, Bemba. It means "dawn" and is taken

behind the currency name *continued*

from the country's nationalist slogan "new dawn of freedom".

Kwanza The official currency of Angola is named either after the Kwanza River or the Bantu word for "first".

Leu Dutch thalers circulating in Romania and Moldova in the 17th century bearing the impression of a lion were widely known as *lei* (lions). A form of the name was kept as a generic term for money (though becoming the lev in Bulgaria).

Lira The Vatican City and Malta retain a currency with a name originating from the value of a troy pound (Latin *libra*) of high purity silver. Turkey's lira shares the same root.

Manat In Azerbaijan and Turkmenistan the currency derives its name from Manah, a goddess of fate and destiny in pre-Islamic Arabia.

Mark An archaic unit of weight for precious metal in Europe equal to eight troy ounces. Germany's mark has been replaced by the euro but Bosnia has its marka and Finland its markka.

Pataca Macau's currency takes its name from a silver coin once popular in Asia, the Mexican eight *reales* or "pieces of eight", known in Portuguese as the Pataca Mexicana.

Peseta Spain's former currency takes its name from the Catalan word *peceta*, meaning "little piece".

Peso The Spanish word for "weight". The main colonial-era coin was worth eight *reales* (the "piece of eight") and was later called the *peso in* Argentina, Chile, Colombia, Cuba, Dominican Republic, Mexico, the Philippines and Uruguay.

Pound The term originates from the value of a troy

pound weight of high purity silver. The symbol is based on a traditional capital "L" with a horizontal line through it, derived from the Latin word *libra*, meaning pound. Sterling dates back to the reign of Henry II in the 12th century and is probably derived from Easterling silver, mined in the area of Germany of the same name. It was famed for the high quality of its silver, which was imported to Britain to form the basis of coinage at the time. Another explanation is that sterling silver's hallmark featured a starling.

Pula In the Setswana language pula means "rain", a scarce and valuable resource in Botswana.

Quetzal Named after the national bird of Guatemala.

Rand South Africa's rand is named after gold-mining area in Transvaal, short for Witwatersrand

Real Brazil's money takes its name from the Portuguese and means "Royal currency". The basic silver unit of Spanish America was the real until about 1860.

Ringgit Malaysia's currency means "jagged" in Malay in reference to the serrated edges of Spanish silver dollars that circulated in the area.

Rouble The name is derived from the Russian word meaning "to chop". Historically, a ruble was a piece of silver chopped off an ingot.

Rupee India's currency takes its name from a Sanskrit word, *rupyah*, meaning "wrought silver".

Yen See Yuan.

Yuan China's currency is taken from the word meaning "round object" in Chinese. Japan's yen is taken from the same source.

Zloty Poland's currency means "golden" in Polish.

Some money *superlatives*

The most valuable coins ...

The highest prices these days are generally paid by American collectors, and often for US coins, the rarest of which can sell for large sums. In 2002 a 1933 gold double eagle ($20) coin was bought by a private collector for $7,590,000 making it the most expensive coin ever sold. The gold double eagle was minted in 1933 but all the coins were recalled and melted down before they were issued, apart from ten which had been stolen by the Mint's chief cashier. These were illegal to own, and federal agents tracked down and recovered nine of them. In a 1996 sting operation the tenth was found, but a few years later permission was given by the American government to allow this (and only this) 1933 double eagle to be privately owned,

> **a 1933 gold double eagle coin was bought for $7,590,000 making it the most expensive coin ever sold**

hence its exceptionally high price. Another coin less than 100 years old – a 1913 Liberty Head nickel, of which only five are known to survive – was sold in June 2005 for $4,150,000. Nine years earlier this same coin had been the first to break the million-dollar price barrier for a rare coin, when it sold in 1996 for $1,485,000.

A Roman gold coin of the usurper emperor Saturninus sold in London for £264,000 in 1996, and six years earlier a unique gold coin made by Brutus, the murderer of Julius Caesar in 44BC, sold for $550,000. However, in 1980, a silver decadrachma of the city of Acragas in Sicily made $572,000. Taking inflation into account, this is the highest price ever realised for an ancient coin. The most valuable medieval coins are sold for similar prices: in 2004 a uniquely important British coin, a gold penny of Coenwulf (796-821), sold for £230,000. Gold coins are always prized, and in June 2005 a 1643 gold Triple Unite of Charles I sold for $431,250. The record price for an Islamic coin was realised in 1998, when a dinar of al-Walid bin 'Abd al-Malik was sold for £308,000.

... and banknotes

Banknotes do not generally fetch such high prices, but six-figure sums have been paid. Rarity, serial number and condition are important in determining the value of a note. For example, a 1937–40 Mauritian 1,000 rupee note with the number A0000 sold at auction in London for £17,250, and a rare 1924 Australian £1,000 note sold in Melbourne for A$86,000. The auction record for an English banknote is £57,200, for a 1797 £1 note sold in 1993. As with coins, rare American banknotes are often more valuable because of the strength of the US market. In 1998 $126,000 was paid for a 1928 $10,000 Federal Reserve note, and in 2005 a $100 Treasury Note from 1890 sold for $356,500.

The biggest banknotes

Ever since their introduction banknotes have remained more or less the same size as they are now, with larger denominations tending to be somewhat bigger than smaller ones. However, in the 19th century notes were certainly larger than the current standard, sometimes up to twice the size. The largest banknotes ever to have been in general circulation are probably Chinese notes of the Ming dynasty: 1,000 cash notes made in the Hungwu reign (1368–98) measured 10 inches by 16 inches (26cm × 40cm). By contrast, the large "white fivers", the old British £5 notes sometimes seen in films of the 1940s and 1950s, which seem so large to modern-day viewers, measured only 8.25 by 5 inches (21cm × 13cm).

The highest denomination coins ...

The earliest Lydian and Greek coins were of a high denomination, being made of electrum, a naturally

some money *superlatives* continued

occurring alloy of gold and silver, and large pieces of silver sometimes weighing up to 8 drachmas (32g). These coins were not intended for everyday use. The highest denomination coin (in real terms) ever made was probably the Mughal emperor Jahangir's 1,000 mohur gold coin (1613), a large gold presentation piece weighing almost 11kg.

In more recent times, an emergency issue of coins in the German state of Westphalia in 1923 included a coin with the value of 1 billion marks, and in 1946 Romania issued a silver coin with a face value of Lei100,000. Modern gold coins can often reach high denominational values. In 1970 Chad issued a Fr20,000 gold piece, and in the same year

a coin with the value of 1 billion marks

South Korea issued a W25,000 gold coin weighing almost 1kg. In 1975 Laos produced a K100,000 coin. In 1990 Greece issued a Dr20,000 coin to celebrate the 50th anniversary of the Italian invasion. These coins are not for everyday circulation and are often made in small quantities for collectors. Only 1,000 of the Greek coins were produced, for example. Of course, high denominations do not necessarily mean high values.

... and banknotes

In the modern world the effects of hyperinflation have produced some remarkably high denomination banknotes. In the early 1920s, Germany produced banknotes in increasingly large numbers and of ever higher values. In 1922

in 1924 notes to the value o 1m million marks were produced

notes of thousands of marks became common, and in 1923 they passed 1m and reached 1 milliard (1,000m). In 1924 notes to the value of 1m million marks were produced. The record for the highest denomination banknote ever produced belongs to Hungary, which in 1946 made a note to the value of 100m billion peng. In Greece in 1944 bank-notes of Dr2,000m, Dr10,000m and Dr100,000m were produced.

More recently, the new states of eastern Europe and the Balkans have indulged in inflationary over-production of paper money. The paper currency of the breakaway Serb Republic in Bosnia quickly descended from sensible denominations of YuD10, YuD50 and YuD100 in 1992 to YuD50m, YuD100m and YuD500m in 1993. In Serbia itself in 1993 notes to the value of YuD500,000m were produced. A currency reform in 1994 rendered 1 new dinar equal to 1,000m old dinars.

The rarest old coins …

Many issues of coin from the ancient world of Greece and Rome are rare, not necessarily because they were made in small quantities but simply because few have survived the accidents of history. Paradoxically, therefore, unique coins are not that unusual. One of the most important, now in the British Museum, is a coin of Octavian (later to become the emperor Augustus) of 28BC, the

❝only seven examples of the 1933 penny are known❞

year when he claimed to be restoring the Roman Republic after 20 years of arbitrary rule and civil war, but was actually establishing himself as monarch. The inscription on the back reads, disingenuously, "He has restored to the People of Rome their laws and rights." Another unique coin of Augustus of 12BC shows the emperor raising a personification of the Roman Republic from her knees – the emperor as saviour of the state.

The usurper Roman emperor Silbannacus (mid-3rd century AD) is known to history solely because of the two surviving coins in his name. He is not mentioned in any ancient source. The existence of another rebel Roman

some money **superlatives** continued

emperor, Domitianus, who ruled Britain for a few days in 271AD, was confirmed in 2003 when a coin bearing his name was found in a hoard in Oxfordshire. One other coin in the name of Domitianus is known, but it was for years dismissed as a hoax.

In the modern world, among the most famous of rare coins is the 1933 British penny, of which only seven examples are known. In 1994 one was sold at auction for £20,000. News of this sale spread throughout the world, exciting the hopes of many who had pennies from 1932 or 1934, years when several million pennies were made. But this cannot compare with the more than $4m paid in 2005 for one of the five known 1913 US Liberty Head nickels.

… and banknotes

Paper money, because of the material from which it is made, has less chance of surviving hundreds, let alone thousands, of years. However, paper money has often been mass-produced in huge quantities and certain notes of some historical periods, such as the American Civil War (1861–65), are still freely available. British banknotes from the 19th and early 20th centuries, particularly in high denominations (£200, £500, £1,000), are often rare and can fetch high prices at auction. The same is true for American high-denomination notes ($500, $1,000) of the same period. There is, for instance, only one known example of the 1891 $1,000 note, and all legal tender issues of 1869 are famously rare. From an earlier period, 14th-century Chinese paper money from the Ming dynasty (1368–1644) is, perhaps understandably given its age, also rare.

Offshore attractions

Offshore banks

2003	No.		No.
Cayman Islands	580	Vanuatu	55
Switzerland	500	Labuan (Malaysia)	54
Bahamas	301	Bahrain	52
Luxembourg	200	Singapore	50
Guernsey	65	Netherlands Antilles	39
Isle of Man	57	Panama	34
Barbados	56		

Source: US Department of State

Tax havens

Andorra	Gibraltar	Nauru
Anguilla	Grenada	Marshall Islands
Antigua & Barbuda	Guernsey	Samoa
Aruba	Isle of Man	San Marino
Bahamas	Jersey	Seychelles
Bahrain	Liberia	St Christopher (St
Barbados	Liechtenstein	Kitts) & Nevis
Belize	Malta	St Lucia
Bermuda	Mauritius	St Vincent & the
British Virgin Islands	Monaco	Grenadines
Cayman Islands	Montserrat	Turks & Caicos
Cook Islands	Netherlands Antilles	US Virgin Islands
Cyprus	Niue	Vanuatu
Dominica	Panama	

Note: A tax haven has three criteria according to the OECD – no or only nominal taxes; lack of effective information exchange; inadequate transparency.
Source: OECD

Notes and coins in circulation

US dollar

	Notes value, $bn	Coins value, $bn
1996	427.1	23.6
1997	458.0	24.3
1998	492.2	25.4
1999	601.2	27.2
2000	563.9	29.9
2001	612.3	31.1
2002	654.8	32.8
2003	690.2	33.9
2004	719.9	34.9
2005	758.3	35.2

Pound

	Notes value, £bn	Notes quantity, bn
2001	27.2	0.98
2002	29.4	0.96
2003	33.9	1.03
2004	36.0	0.89
2005	35.4	0.74

Euro

	Notes value, €bn	Coins value, €bn
2002	358.5	12.4
2003	435.1	14.1
2004	501.3	15.4
2005	565.2	15.6
2006*	580.1	17.2

*As of June.

Sources: Financial Management Service, US Treasury; Bank of England; European Central Bank

Euros printed

Banknotes produced by Jan 1st 2002

	Quantity, m	Denomination	Quantity, m
Germany	4,342	5	2,415
France	2,570	10	3,013
Italy	2,380	20	3,608
Spain	1,924	50	3,674
Netherlands	655	100	1,246
Greece	581	200	229
Portugal	535	500	360
Belgium	530	Total	14,545
Austria	520		
Ireland	243		
Finland	219		
Luxembourg	46		
Total	14,545		

Source: European Central Bank

The life of $ and £ notes

$	Months, av.	£	Months, av.
1	21.3	5	12
5	24.4	10	36–48
10	25.0	20	36–48
20	21.8	50	60–120
50	55.4		
100	60.4		

Sources: Federal Reserve; Bank of England

Exchange rates

Period average	$1 = €	$1 = £	$1 = ¥
1950	na	0.36	361.10
1960	0.63	0.36	360.00
1965	0.63	0.36	360.00
1970	0.66	0.42	360.00
1975	0.56	0.45	296.79
1980	0.65	0.43	226.74
1985	1.33	0.77	238.54
1990	0.77	0.56	144.79
1995	0.75	0.63	94.06
2000	1.09	0.66	107.77
2001	1.18	0.69	121.53
2002	1.06	0.67	125.39
2003	0.89	0.61	115.93
2004	0.81	0.55	108.19
2005	0.80	0.55	110.22

Period average	$ = €1	$ = £1	$ = ¥1
1950	na	2.80	0.0028
1960	1.59	2.80	0.0028
1965	1.59	2.80	0.0028
1970	1.52	2.40	0.0028
1975	1.79	2.22	0.0034
1980	1.54	2.33	0.0044
1985	0.75	1.30	0.0042
1990	1.30	1.78	0.0069
1995	1.33	1.58	0.0106
2000	0.92	1.52	0.0093
2001	0.85	1.44	0.0082
2002	0.94	1.50	0.0080
2003	1.12	1.63	0.0086
2004	1.23	1.83	0.0092
2005	1.24	1.82	0.0091

Note: Synthetic $/€ rate until 1999.

Sources: IMF: International Financial Statistics; Thomson Datastream

Exchange-rate pegs

Exchange rates can be tied to a particular currency as a currency union (eg, the countries in the euro area) or individually (eg, fixed to the US$). A peg reduces volatility, but it also reduces flexibility in monetary policy.

Euro currency members

Austria	Germany	Luxembourg
Belgium	Greece	Netherlands
Finland	Ireland	Portugal
France	Italy	Spain

Non-members pegged to the euro: Bosnia, Bulgaria, Cyprus, Denmark, Estonia, Hungary, Latvia, Lithuania, Malta, Slovakia, Slovenia

CFA franc zone, pegged to the euro

Benin	Congo-Brazzaville	Mali
Burkina Faso	Côte d'Ivoire	Niger
Cameroon	Equatorial Guinea	Senegal
Central African Rep.	Gabon	Togo
Chad	Guinea-Bissau	

Countries with currencies pegged to US$

Bahamas	Jordan	Panama
Bahrain	Kuwait	Qatar
Barbados	Lebanon	Saudi Arabia
Belize	Maldives	Seychelles
Ecuador	Micronesia	Syria
El Salvador	Netherlands Antilles	UAE
Eritrea	Oman	Venezuela

Eastern Caribbean Currency Union, pegged to the US$

Antigua & Barbuda	Grenada	St Lucia
Dominica	St Kitts & Nevis	St Vincent & the Grenadines

Source: IMF, as at December 2005

The changing world economy

Shares of world GDP at purchasing-power parity exchange rates, %

	1820	1870	1913	1950	1973	1998	2005*
Western Europe	23.6	33.6	33.5	26.3	25.7	20.6	19
US, Canada, Australia, New Zealand	1.9	10.2	21.7	30.6	25.3	25.1	24
Japan	3.0	2.3	2.6	3.0	7.7	7.7	6
China	32.9	17.2	8.9	4.5	4.6	11.5	14
Other Asia	23.3	18.8	13.0	11.0	11.8	18.0	20
Latin America	2.0	2.5	4.5	7.9	8.7	8.7	8
Central and eastern Europe	8.8	11.7	13.1	13.1	12.9	5.3	6
Africa	4.5	3.7	2.7	3.6	3.3	3.1	3
World	100.0	100.0	100.0	100.0	100.0	100.0	100.0

* Estimated.
Sources: *The World Economy* by Angus Maddison; IMF

GDP per person, PPP$, 1990 prices

	1820	1870	1913	1950	1973	1998	2005*
US	1,257	2,445	5,301	9,561	16,689	27,331	31,200
UK	1,707	3,191	4,921	6,907	12,022	18,714	21,900
France	1,230	1,876	3,485	5,270	13,123	19,558	21,800
Japan	669	737	1,387	1,926	11,439	20,413	21,800
Germany	1,058	1,821	3,648	3,881	11,966	17,799	19,200
Italy	1,117	1,499	2,564	3,502	10,643	17,759	19,100
Spain	1,063	1,376	2,255	2,397	8,739	14,227	17,400
China	600	530	552	439	839	3,117	5,400
India	533	533	673	619	853	1,746	2,300
World	667	867	1,510	2,114	4,104	5,709	6,800

* Estimated.
Note: GDP is the sum of all output produced by economic activity. PPP statistics adjust for cost of living differences by replacing normal exchange rates with rates designed to equalise the prices of a standard "basket" of goods and services.
Sources: *The World Economy* by Angus Maddison; IMF; World Bank

Leading exporters

Biggest visible traders
% of world visible exports, 2004

Euro area	15.61	Spain	2.05
Germany	10.11	Russia	2.04
US	9.02	Taiwan	1.92
China	6.60	Switzerland	1.54
Japan	5.99	Malaysia	1.41
France	4.68	Saudi Arabia	1.40
Italy	3.92	Sweden	1.39
UK	3.89	Austria	1.25
Canada	3.67	Ireland	1.11
Chile	3.56	Singapore	1.10
Netherlands	3.38	India	1.09
South Korea	2.87	Brazil	1.07
Belgium	2.73	Thailand	1.07
Mexico	2.09	UAE	1.01

Biggest invisible traders
% of world invisible exports, 2004

Euro area	19.26	China	2.11
US	18.30	Canada	1.96
UK	11.12	Austria	1.72
Germany	6.98	Sweden	1.72
France	5.68	Singapore	1.44
Japan	5.36	South Korea	1.27
Netherlands	3.54	Denmark	1.25
Italy	3.48	India	1.17
Switzerland	2.92	Taiwan	1.04
Spain	2.90	Australia	1.00
Hong Kong	2.65	Norway	0.98
Belgium	2.43	Greece	0.92
Ireland	2.40	Russia	0.78
Luxembourg	2.40	Turkey	0.68

Sources: IMF; WTO; national statistics

Foreign direct investment

Inflows, $bn

	1992–97 ave.	2000	2001	2002	2003	2004	Stocks, % of GDP, end 2004
EU15	95.8	671.4	357.4	397.1	326.6	196.1	31.3
EU25				420.4	338.7	216.4	31.7
Other western Europe	5.0	26.0	11.4	7.1	20.7	7.0	37.4
North America	68.3	380.8	186.9	92.8	63.2	102.2	14.0
Other developed countries	11.7	29.8	15.7	27.4	19.6	54.5	7.9
Africa	5.9	8.7	19.6	13.0	18.0	18.1	27.8
Latin America & the Caribbean	38.2	97.5	88.1	50.5	46.9	67.5	34.1
Other Asia	74.5	146.2	112.0	92.0	101.4	147.6	23.2
Central & eastern Europe	11.5	27.5	26.4	12.8	24.1	34.9	21.5
Total	310.9	1387.9	817.5	716.1	632.6	648.1	21.7

Developing economies with the biggest inflows in 2004, $bn

	1992–97 ave.	2000	2001	2002	2003	2004	Stocks, % of GDP, end 2004
China	32.8	40.7	46.9	52.7	53.5	60.6	14.9
Hong Kong	7.8	61.9	23.8	9.7	13.6	34.0	277.6
Brazil	6.6	32.8	22.5	16.6	10.1	18.2	25.2
Mexico	9.6	16.6	26.8	15.1	11.4	16.6	27.0
Singapore	8.3	17.2	15.0	5.8	9.3	16.1	150.2
Russia	2.0	2.7	2.5	3.5	8.0	11.7	16.9
South Korea	1.3	8.6	3.7	3.0	3.8	7.7	10.7
Chile	2.9	4.9	4.2	2.6	4.4	7.6	58.2

Note: Foreign direct investment (FDI) is long-term investment in companies in a foreign country, implying a certain degree of control of those companies. Stocks indicate the value of those investments.

Source: United Nations Conference on Trade and Development

Sending money home

Workers overseas send about $100 billion back to their home country each year, and it is growing at double-digit rates. India received over $20 billion from overseas in 2003, nearly double the 2000 amount. The Philippines received $9 billion in 2004, compared with only $125m in 2000. Mexico has more than doubled its inflow, to over $16 billion. Other rapidly growing recipients are China (eight times the 2000 amount) and Guatemala (more than four times).

Countries' receipts, $bn	2000	2001	2002	2003	2004
India	12.7	14.2	15.6	21.6	na
Mexico	6.6	8.9	9.8	13.4	16.6
Philippines	0.1	0.1	0.2	8.2	9.0
Spain	3.4	3.7	4.0	4.7	5.2
China	0.6	0.9	1.7	3.3	4.6
Morocco	2.2	3.3	2.9	3.6	4.2
Pakistan	1.1	1.5	3.6	4.0	3.9
Bangladesh	2.0	2.1	2.8	3.2	3.6
Egypt	2.9	2.9	2.9	3.0	3.3
Colombia	1.6	2.0	2.5	3.1	3.2
Portugal	3.2	3.3	2.7	2.8	3.0
Guatemala	0.6	0.6	1.6	2.1	2.6
El Salvador	1.8	1.9	1.9	2.1	2.5
Brazil	1.1	1.2	1.7	2.0	2.5
Poland	1.5	1.8	1.7	2.3	2.3
Nigeria	1.4	1.2	1.2	1.1	2.3
Dominican Republic	1.7	1.8	2.0	2.1	2.2
Jordan	1.7	1.8	1.9	2.0	2.1
Indonesia	1.2	1.0	1.3	1.5	1.7
Ecuador	1.3	1.4	1.4	1.5	1.6

Source: World Bank

Interest rates

Short-term rates

London interbank offer rates, %

	US	UK	Japan	Euro area
1979	12.09	13.88	6.08	…
1980	14.19	16.35	11.30	…
1981	16.87	14.32	7.73	…
1982	13.29	12.58	6.99	…
1983	9.72	10.18	6.57	…
1984	10.94	10.02	6.43	…
1985	8.40	12.25	6.68	…
1986	6.86	10.97	5.12	…
1987	7.18	9.80	4.26	…
1988	7.98	10.36	4.51	…
1989	9.28	13.94	5.46	…
1990	8.31	14.79	7.76	…
1991	5.99	11.67	7.38	…
1992	3.86	9.70	4.46	…
1993	3.29	6.06	3.00	…
1994	4.74	5.54	2.31	…
1995	6.04	6.73	1.27	…
1996	5.51	6.09	0.63	…
1997	5.76	6.90	0.63	…
1998	5.57	7.39	0.72	…
1999	5.41	5.54	0.22	2.96
2000	6.53	6.19	0.28	4.41
2001	3.78	5.04	0.15	4.26
2002	1.80	4.06	0.08	3.32
2003	1.22	3.73	0.06	2.33
2004	1.62	4.64	0.05	2.11
2005	4.49	4.64	0.07	2.47
2006 May	5.18	4.70	0.19	2.89

Source: Thomson Datastream

Some notable highs Money-market interest rates in Argentina averaged nearly 1.4m% in 1989 and over 9m% in 1990. Russian rates averaged 190% in 1995. Zimbabwe's rates averaged over 100% in 2003 and 2004. Turkey's interbank money-market rate came down from an average of 92% in 2001 to 13.25% in early 2006.

Central bank rates

America The US federal funds rate went from 4.75% in 1977 to 19% in 1981. Its next low point was 3% in 1993 before going up to 6.5% in 2000. The 45-year low point of 1% ran from June 2003 to June 2004, then rising in 17 quarter-point moves to 5.25% by June 2006.

Britain The UK's minimum lending rate went to 15% in 1976, down to 5% in 1977 then up to 17% in 1979. MLR was replaced with the "Minimum Bank 1 Dealing Rate" in August 1981. This came down to below 8% in 1988. On Black Wednesday (September 16th 1992) the rate went briefly up to 15%. The repo rate, which became the new official rate in May 1997, went to a low of 3.5% in July 2003 then rose in five quarter-point stages to 4.75% in August 2004. A year later it came down to 4.50%.

Japan The Bank of Japan's official discount rate was set at a high of 9% in 1973 and again in 1980. It has been 0.10% since September 2001. After six years of a zero-rate policy, the bank raised the key overnight call rate to 0.25% in July 2006.

Sources: IMF; Federal Reserve; Bank of England; Bank of Japan

Corporate tax rates

Average, %

	1998	2006	% change, 1998–2006
Argentina	33.00	35.00	6.06
Australia	36.00	30.00	-16.67
Austria	34.00	25.00	-26.47
Bangladesh	40.00	30.00	-25.00
Belgium	40.17	33.99	-15.38
Bolivia	25.00	25.00	0.00
Brazil	25.00	34.00*	36.00
Canada	44.60	36.10	-19.06
Chile	15.00	17.00	13.33
China	33.00	33.00	0.00
Colombia	35.00	35.00	0.00
Costa Rica	30.00	30.00	0.00
Czech Republic	35.00	24.00	-31.43
Denmark	34.00	28.00	-17.65
Dominican Republic	25.00	30.00	20.00
Ecuador†	36.25	20.00	-44.83
Finland	28.00	26.00	-7.14
France	41.66	33.33	-20.00
Germany	50.13	38.34	-23.52
Greece†	37.50	25.50	-32.00
Hong Kong	16.50	17.50	6.06
Hungary	18.00	16.00	-11.11
Iceland‡	33.00	18.00	-45.45
India	35.00	33.66	-3.83
Indonesia	30.00	30.00	0.00
Ireland	32.00	12.50†	-60.94
Italy	41.25	37.25	-9.70
Japan	51.60	40.69	-21.14
Luxembourg	37.45	29.63	-20.88
Malaysia	28.00	28.00	0.00
Mexico	34.00	29.00	-14.71
Mozambique	35.00	32.00	-8.57
Netherlands†	33.00	27.55	-16.52
New Zealand	28.00	33.00	17.86

Norway	30.00	28.00	-6.67
Pakistan	37.00	35.00	-5.41
Panama	25.00	30.00	20.00
Papua New Guinea	30.00	30.00	0.00
Peru	30.00	30.00	0.00
Philippines	34.00	35.00	2.94
Poland	36.00	19.00	-47.22
Portugal	37.40	27.50	-26.47
Russia	na	24.00	na
Singapore	26.00	20.00	-23.08
South Africa	na	36.90	na
South Korea	30.80	27.50	-10.71
Spain	35.00	35.00	0.00
Sri Lanka	35.00	32.50	-7.14
Sweden	28.00	28.00	0.00
Switzerland	27.80	21.30	-23.38
Taiwan	na	25.00	na
Thailand	30.00	30.00	0.00
Turkey	44.00	30.00	-31.82
UK	31.00	30.00	-3.23
Ukraine	na	25.00	na
Uruguay	30.00	30.00	0.00
US	40.00	40.00	0.00
Venezuela	34.00	34.00	0.00
Vietnam	32.50	28.00	-13.85

*Includes social contribution tax on profits.   †Average rate from a tax band.
‡Applies to limited liability companies only.
Source: KPMG

Average corporate tax rates by region, %

	OECD	EU	Latin America	Asia-Pacific
1998	35.67	36.17	32.03	32.30
2000	34.10	35.44	29.30	32.10
2002	31.39	32.53	30.20	31.05
2004	29.96	31.32	30.02	30.37
2006	28.31	25.04	28.25	29.99

Source: KPMG

What companies pay in tax

Total, $bn

	1970	1980	1990	2000	2004
Australia	1.62	5.52	12.86	25.18	27.94*
Canada	3.04	10.04	14.73	32.08	35.32
France	3.15	14.22	27.85	40.68	56.18
Germany	3.45	16.88	26.58	34.16	43.01
Ireland	0.11	0.30	0.79	3.58	6.62
Italy	1.84	10.65	43.00	31.57	47.97
Japan	10.83	60.07	202.29	173.70	167.06
South Korea	na	1.22	6.72	17.04	23.95
Spain	0.52	2.60	14.93	18.06	35.89
Sweden	0.59	1.50	4.00	9.69	10.73
Switzerland	0.37	1.81	4.69	6.77	8.77
UK	3.98	15.76	35.43	52.52	61.73
US	36.57	78.62	140.61	254.98	258.32

Per head of population, $

	1970	1980	1990	2000	2004
Australia	126	373	749	1,307	1,397*
Canada	142	410	532	1,045	971*
France	61	258	479	671	904
Germany	57	274	420	416	521
Ireland	36	87	224	942	1,632
Italy	34	189	758	547	721*
Japan	104	514	1,637	1,369	1,118*
South Korea	–	32	157	362	498
Spain	15	69	381	449	842
Sweden	74	181	467	1,093	1,193
Switzerland	59	284	690	939	1,092*
UK	72	280	619	892	840*
US	178	345	562	903	776*

*2003

Source: OECD

What individuals pay in tax

Total, $bn

	1970	1980	1990	2000	2004
Australia	3.56	19.96	39.08	44.89	64.19*
Canada	8.73	29.46	85.47	96.73	116.13
France	5.37	32.19	55.74	106.09	151.65
Germany	16.20	91.61	151.67	178.90	216.60
Ireland	0.22	2.09	5.06	9.12	15.18
Italy	3.05	31.52	112.57	115.62	180.94
Japan	8.84	66.94	251.36	266.09	210.51
South Korea	na	1.26	10.51	17.64	22.80
Spain	0.73	10.40	36.77	37.56	64.94
Sweden	6.67	25.15	49.19	42.31	54.67
Switzerland	1.64	11.14	23.81	26.17	37.08
UK	14.44	55.47	105.87	158.26	223.68
US	101.27	285.51	582.82	1,223.59	1,028.55

Per head of population, $

	1970	1980	1990	2000	2004
Australia	277	1,348	2,276	2,329	3,210*
Canada	409	1,202	3,086	3,152	3,231*
France	103	584	958	1,749	2,439
Germany	267	1,488	2,398	2,177	2,625
Ireland	75	616	1,442	2,400	3,739*
Italy	57	558	1,985	2,002	2,734*
Japan	85	573	2,035	2,096	1,503*
South Korea	–	33	245	375	474
Spain	21	275	939	933	1,523
Sweden	829	3,027	5,747	4,769	6,079
Switzerland	262	1,745	3,504	3,630	4,404*
UK	260	985	1,850	2,688	3,078*
US	494	1,254	2,330	4,332	3,396*

*2003
Source: OECD

How taxing for top earners?

Top personal income tax rate, %

	1975	1980	1985	1995	2000	2005
Australia	65.0	na	60.0	47.0	47.0	47.0
Austria	62.0	62.0	62.0	50.0	50.0	50.0
Belgium	60.0	76.3	71.6	55.0	55.0	50.0
Canada	47.0	na	34.0	29.0	29.0	29.0
France	60.0	60.0	65.0	na	53.0	48.0
Germany	56.0	56.0	56.0	53.0	51.0	42.0
Greece	63.0	60.0	63.0	45.0	45.0	40.0
Ireland	77.0	60.0	65.0	48.0	44.0	42.0
Italy	72.0	72.0	65.0	51.0	45.0	43.0
Japan	75.0	93.0	70.0	50.0	37.0	37.0
Luxembourg	57.0	58.4	57.0	50.0	46.0	38.0
Mexico	na	55.0	55.0	35.0	40.0	30.0
Netherlands	71.0	72.0	72.0	60.0	60.0	52.0
New Zealand	60.0	60.0	66.0	33.0	39.0	39.0
Norway	73.0	na	40.0	13.7	29.0	27.0
Portugal	na	na	60.0	40.0	40.0	40.0
South Korea	na	na	55.0	45.0	40.0	35.0
Spain	62.0	65.5	66.0	56.0	40.0	29.0
Sweden	87.0	na	80.0	30.0	25.0	25.0
Switzerland	44.0	na	11.5	11.5	12.0	12.0
UK	83.0	na	60.0	40.0	40.0	40.0
US (Federal data)	70.0	70.0	50.0	39.6	40.0	35.0

Sources: OECD; The Tax Policy Centre, Urban Institute, Brookings Institution

Wealth and debt

Net wealth as % of disposable income

	1994	2005
Italy	748.0	960.6*
US	480.4	771.1
UK	543.9	755.0*
Japan	766.5	724.9*
France	471.8	576.5
Germany	486.4	572.2*
Canada	477.3	520.4

*2004

Note. Net wealth is defined as non-financial and financial assets minus liabilities (consumer debt);
Non-financial assets include stock of durable goods at replacement cost & dwellings at market value.
Financial assets comprise currency & deposits, securities (except shares), loans, shares and other
equity, insurance technical reserves.

Consumer debt as % of disposable income

	1994	2005
UK	107.5	155.1*
Japan	132.2	131.8*
US	91.8	131.8
Canada	103.1	127.6
Germany	97.0	108.2*
France	80.7	91.1
Italy	31.9	54.7*

*2004
Source: OECD

Great business books

Here is a list of 20 business books that stand out from the crowd that have been published over the years.

Barbarians at the Gate
Bryan Burrough and John Helyar, 1990
The fall of RJR Nabisco

Built to Last
Jim Collins and Jerry Porras, 1994
What it takes to endure

Competitive Strategy
Michael Porter, 1980
How to gain competitive advantage

Corporate Strategy
Igor Ansoff, 1965
The ABC of strategic planning

The Dilbert Principle
Scott Adams, 1996
The foolish ways of managers

Future Shock
Alvin Tofler, 1970
Fast change is traumatic and inevitable

The Human Side of Enterprise
Douglas McGregor, 1960
The origin of Theories X and Y

In Search of Excellence
Tom Peters and Robert Waterman, 1982
Boosting the ego of corporate America

Liar's Poker
Michael Lewis, 1990
Wall Street laid bare

The Machine that Changed the World
James Womack, Dan Jones and Daniel Roos, 1991
The story of lean production

Microserfs
Douglas Coupland, 1995
Get a life in Silicon Valley

My Years with General Motors
Alfred Sloan, 1963
How GM was built – by the man who did it

The One Minute Manager
Kenneth Blanchard and Spencer Johnson, 1981
Keep it simple ... and swift

The Peter Principle
L.J. Peter and R. Hull, 1969
The rise of the incompetent

The Principles of Scientific Management
Frederick Winslow Taylor, 1911
The very first business bestseller

Re-engineering the Corporation
Michael Hammer and James Champy, 1993
Revolution through process design

Small is Beautiful
E.F. Schumacher, 1973
The title says it all

The Smartest Guys in the Room
Bethany McLean and Peter Elkind, 2003
The best telling of the scandalous fall of Enron

Strategy and Structure
Alfred Chandler, 1962
Why structure follows strategy

Up the Organisation
Robert Townsend, 1970
Ex-Avis boss teaches the world how to try harder

Compiled by Tim Hindle

LATIN **that lawyers like to use**

A fortiori	for a compelling reason
Ad valorem	value
Affidavit	he has said it (a sworn statement)
Bona fide	in good faith, honestly, sincerely, without deception (**Mala fide** in bad faith)
Bona vacantia	vacant goods; goods without an owner
Caveat emptor	buyer beware
De minimis non curat lex	the law is not concerned with trivial matters
De facto	in point of fact
Eiusdem generis	of the same kind
Ex gratia	as a favour; without liability
Ex parte	on behalf of one party
Fieri facias	make it happen
Functus officio	having shot one's bolt; spent
Habeas corpus	let him have his body back
Ignorantia legis non excusat	ignorance of the law is not an excuse
In flagrante delicto	in the act of committing a crime
In personam	in respect of the person; personally
In re	in the matter of
In rem	in respect of the thing; reality
Inter alia	among other things
Inter partes	between the parties
Inter vivos	between living people
Intra vires	within the permitted powers
Ipso facto	by the very fact itself
Lex fori	the law of the place where the case is being heard
Lex loci	the law of the place where the act was done
Locus standi	official standing; recognition

Mala in se	wrongs in themselves
Mala prohibita	forbidden wrongs
Mandamus	we command
Mens rea	guilty mind
Mutatis mutandis	change and change about
Nemine contradicente (nem. con.)	with no one speaking against
Nemo dat quod non habet (nemo dat)	no one can give what he does not have
Nolle prosequi	do not pursue
Non est factum	it is not his act (he didn't mean to do it)
Obiter dicta	incidental comments
Pari passu	of equal power
Prima facie	on the face of it
Per diem	by the day; an allowance paid businessmen to cover daily expenses while travelling
Pro rata	for the rate; divided in proportion
Pro tempore	for the time being; sometimes shortened to pro tem
Quantum meruit	as much as he deserves
Quid pro quo	something for something (you scratch my back, I'll scratch yours)
Ratio decidendi	the reason for deciding
Res ipsa loquitur	it speaks for itself
Sine die	without specifying a day
Sine qua non	without which, not (anything indispensable)
Sub judice	under adjudication
Sui generis	of its own kind
Uberrimae fidei	of the utmost good faith
Ultra vires	outside the permitted powers
Verbatim	word-for-word; a precise rendering of a discussion or text

What's in a WORD

Many terms and expressions are used in business without people giving a second thought to how they have come about. Here are the origins of some popular ones.

Acid test A term meaning to test the true worth of something is derived from the practice of testing the purity of gold with nitric acid in the days when it was used as a currency.

Bear A speculator who sells securities in the expectation that prices will fall. Bears may sell short, ie, sell securities they do not own, leading to suggestions that the expression refers to the phrase "selling the skin before you have caught the bear". Trappers were also in the habit of short selling their wares. Short sellers were called "bearskin jobbers" in 18th century London.

Bellwether The term for a closely watched company that indicates the fortunes of an entire industry takes its name from castrated male sheep that lead flocks. These sheep used to wear bells to help shepherds find them in the dark or in bad weather.

Benchmark The technique for comparing performance in business and finance refers to a surveyor's mark made on a stationary object for use as a reference point for subsequent observations.

Big cheese Important people may have derived their epithet from colonial India. The Urdu word "*chiz*", which means thing, like so many other phrases was taken up by the British. Its meaning was altered to mean "good".

Bite the bullet Taking a difficult decision is probably less painful than suffering an operation without anaesthetic. Before modern pain-killing drugs were available soldier were given a bullet to bite to stop cries of agony during surgery.

Blue chip An American term referring to the colour of the highest value poker chip.

Boss The Dutch word "*baas*", meaning master, was adopted in America from Dutch colonisers and in South Africa by the British from the Afrikaners.

The buck stops here American poker players in the 19th century would use a bit of buckshot to denote which player was the dealer and so had ultimate responsibility to pass out the cards.

Bull An investor who buys hoping that prices will rise. Probably named just to contrast them with bears. Bull and bear baiting were popular sports in Britain at the time that the forerunner of the modern stockmarket emerged.

Cash cow Came into common usage only recently but the term milch cow was used as early as the 17th century to mean a dependable source of prosperity.

Dead cat bounce A small improvement in a bear market is so called because "even dead cats bounce".

Dead wood Someone or something serving no purpose, taken from a technique in shipbuilding. Timbers were laid on the keel for no other reason that to make it a little more rigid.

Line your pockets It has been suggested that the term originates from the practice of tailors in Regency England to send garments to George "Beau" Brummell stuffed with banknotes in order to seek the patronage of the famous dandy and fashion leader.

Pac-Man strategy A measure to avoid takeover whereby the intended target counterattacks by making an offer for the firm that is trying to acquire it, named after the 1980s arcade game.

Pay through the nose The Danes of the 9th century imposed a "nose" tax on the Irish, so-called because those who avoided paying had their nostrils slit.

what's in a word *continued*

Poison pill An anti-takeover measure that attempts to make the potential acquiree a less attractive target, named after the cyanide pills that enemy agents swallow in the event of capture.

Red tape British lawyers and government officials formerly used to bind documents together with red cloth tape. The term was first used to describe bureaucracy by Charles Dickens.

Smart Alec The term was originally non-pejorative and is thought to derive from an American conman, Alec Hoag. He perfected a method for stealing from the unsuspecting clients of prostitutes by using a sliding panel to hide in the room while a hooker and customer went about their business. He later emerged to remove wallets and watches while the punter slept, supposedly a considerable improvement on the previous preferred method of bursting in while the satisfied client slept.

Stag Someone who applies for an allotment of shares in an initial public offering, with a view to selling them straight away at a healthy premium. It is suggested that the term originates because stag is also a term used for a castrated bull.

Tycoon Wealthy and successful businessmen get their names from the Japanese "*taikun*", a powerful military leader. The word became popular in the early part of the 20th century.

White knight A friendly potential buyer of a firm that is threatened by a less welcome suitor. In *Alice through the Looking Glass* the heroine is captured by the red knight but is rescued at once by the white knight.

Brand names that entered the language

Aspirin Bayer still owns the trademark for the acetylated derivative of salicylic acid in many countries.

AstroTurf Commonly applied to any artificial grass surface. AstroTurf, developed by Monsanto industries, was originally called Chemgrass.

Band Aid The original plastic adhesive plaster was developed by Johnson & Johnson.

Biro The original ball-point pen, invented by a Hungarian, Laszlo Biro, in 1938 is the name given to all such writing implements today. The patent was acquired by BIC Crystal.

Bubble Wrap Transparent air-pocket-filled plastic sheeting for wrapping fragile goods is also great fun to pop by hand. The term for the genuine article is a trademark of the Sealed Air Corporation.

Breathalyser The instrument for police checks for alcohol consumed by a suspect driver is a trademark of Draeger Safety.

Coke The common name for any cola-based soft drink is still a trademark of Coca-Cola.

Filofax At the height of their popularity in the 1980s, before electronic devices took over, any leather-bound personal organiser was known as a Filofax. The Filofax company had made the products since1921.

Frisbee Of the many varieties of flying disk available, only Wham-O owns the brand name and registered trademark of Frisbee.

Google The internet search engine has become a verb. To google means to obtain information from the internet by whatever means.

brand names *continued*

Hoover Was once a synonym for vacuum cleaners and even made it as a verb. The Hoover Company has been making the devices since 1907.

Hula-Hoop The twirling hoop around hips or knees is a Hula-Hoop only if made by Wham-O.

Jacuzzi Only the whirlpool baths made by the company founded by Roy Jacuzzi can rightfully bear the name.

Jeep Rugged four-wheel drive vehicles may not bear the name unless they are made by Jeep, which began producing the original vehicles for the American army in the second world war. DaimlerChrysler now owns Jeep.

Jet Ski Small motorised personal watercraft are commonly known as Jet Skis, although the term is a brand name owned by Kawasaki Heavy Industries of Japan.

Kitty Litter Felines in search of relief indoors must thank Edward Lowe, who invented the cat-box filler in 1947.

Kleenex The brand name of Kimberley-Clark's product has become synonymous with paper tissues around the world.

Linoleum Patented in England by Frederick Walton in 1860 and giving its name to almost any man-made flexible floorage material, lino, like escalator and harmonica, had a trademark that has long-since elapsed but the generic term remains.

Muzak Anonymous, bland and faintly irritating background music heard in shops and other public places may genuinely be called Muzak only if produced by the South Carolina-based company of the same name.

Rawlplug In 1919 Rawlings invented a fibre or plastic plug that allows the insertion of a screw into a hole drilled into masonry. The company, which is still in existence, now competes with dozens of competitors to produce the devices to which it has lent its name.

Rollerblade The Rollerblade company that started the craze for in-line rollerskating can claim the trademark.

Scotch Tape Transparent cellophane adhesive tape is widely known as Scotch tape in America though the name is a trademark of the 3M company. In Britain the product is known as Sellotape, another brand name now owned by Henkel Consumer Adhesives.

Styrofoam Expanded polystyrene is often called Styrofoam though the word is a trade name of the Dow Chemical Company.

Teflon The trade name for a solid, chemically inert polymer of tetrafluoroethylene manufactured by Dupont rather than any non-stick coating on cooking utensils.

Thermos The first vacuum flasks were made Germany in 1904 by Thermos GmbH. The tradename for their flasks is still registered.

Tupperware Plastic storage boxes produced by any firm other than the Tupperware Corporation have no right to take that name.

Vaseline Petroleum jelly produced by Unilever is known as Vaseline. Anything else is just plain petroleum jelly.

Walkman Mobile personal stereo systems not produced by Sony cannot properly bear the name.

Xerox Photocopiers of any stripe were routinely known as Xerox machines for many years. The financial plight of the company and its slide out of the world's offices has all but stopped the practice.

Business "jargon"

"Incomprehensible jargon is the hallmark of a profession," said Kingman Brewster, a former president of Yale University. He had in mind venerable professions such as medicine, the law and banking, professions whose practitioners have devised a language that can be incomprehensible to all but other practitioners. He was not, in all probability, referring to the profession that arguably has the most jargon of them all: the management profession.

Managers gathered round the coffee machine say things to each other such as: "There's been a paradigm shift. We must identify new synergies for our organisational capabilities." No other manager is going to admit to not understanding what this means. The outsider, though, might wonder why they did not simply say: "Things have changed a lot lately. We need to do better in the future."

Problems start to escalate when managers from different departments talk to each other. For each has its own sub-language, and these days the IT people have the richest. They want to talk in real time or offline, and

they're always in search of solutions – leading-edge solutions, that is

they are limited only by their intellectual bandwidth. They are always talking about the drivers of their business (mainly digitisation), and they like to use leading-edge technology in order to create multifunctional new products and services that are networked throughout the organisation. Going forward, they're always in search of solutions – leading-edge solutions, that is.

The human-resources folks, on the other hand, have issues on their agendas. They talk about the right skill sets, and doing 360-degree evaluations of the talent (sounds uncomfortable). Talent on the fast track these days has to be a good team player, or a knowledge harvester. Value creators have to work in cross-functional teams and try to put themselves in win-win situations, ones in which it seems to be possible for neither side to lose. Whatever that is, it's certainly not cricket.

For the marketing division everything is a brand. According to one typology, there is a familiarity brand, a distraction brand and a muscle brand. Brands are stretched, extended and built upon, while brand new brands are launched with carefully targeted campaigns. A niche brand has its own socioeconomic dynamic, of course.

Business jargon is susceptible to fashion. One of today's celebrated themes is risk. Managers know that there are no certainties any more, that everything is changing. Change is constant and increasing; they recite it like a mantra.

So too is risk. Everywhere managers look now they find risk – financial risk, structural risk, strategic risk, operational risk – the list is endless. All this risk has to be controlled in a proactive value-creating way. One recent book has a chapter

all this risk has to be controlled in a proactive value-creating way

headed "Managing Programme Risk". Do not be misled. It has nothing to do with hanging on to pieces of paper at the theatre.

Then there is knowledge. Managers live in a knowledge economy full of knowledge-intensive firms. Knowledge management is everybody's ideal core competence – although according to one author "we cannot understand KM (yes, it already has its own acronym) in terms of broad structural drivers." In what terms, you might be tempted to ask, can we understand it?

Acronyms and abbreviations are everywhere. Most of them are three-letter specimens (TQM, BPR, JIT, ABC,

business "jargon" continued

CRM, CIO and CTO, for a start), though occasionally the rarer two- and four-letter specimens can be found – IT and KM, for example, or MBWA and RFID. Some are known widely among managers, but some are home-made, a sort of secret code among a small exclusive group. "Told JP we'd do the FV before we head for LA" sort of thing.

Another fashionable subject with a rich seam of jargon is leadership. Leadership, we are told, is about empowerment and mastering capabilities. Management guru Tom Peters, in a recent book, *Re-Imagine*, says that leadership is "an act called conveying the Brand Promise via demonstrated High Conviction in pursuit of Great Purpose". Management writers love using capital letters; they think it helps simple-minded readers get IT.

Leaders these days are forever making journeys. Often they are journeys of self-discovery where they can relate to their inner selves. Examples from history are frequently called upon. Famous journey-takers, such as Alexander the Great and Shackleton, are hardy favourites. One leadership book about Queen Elizabeth I says that when the good queen "seemed to vacillate, it was likely because the analytical and intuitive aspects of a pending decision were not in sync in terms of the action itself or its timing". Does that mean that the CEO of Elizabethan England Inc could not make up her mind?

Jargon becomes a problem when managers fail to recognise times when it is appropriate and times when it is not. What to make of this, for example, taken from the home page of a very large service company's website: "Customized solutions boost employee productivity and satisfaction, while supporting effective program management and cost control. Our focus on service excellence, technology investment, and Six Sigma measurement standards ensures consistent results-driven performance. Clients receive continual information on best practices, cost-reduction opportunities, and competitive program enhancements, while our consultants provide each employee with resourceful and responsive personal advocacy." This is a sort of uber-jargon, expressed in such an

> **a sort of uber-jargon, expressed in such an Orwellian dead-pan tone that it is not even funny**

Orwellian dead-pan tone that it is not even funny. The origin of the word "jargon" may well have been an ancient word for the incomprehensible twittering of birds. There are many birds that cannot twitter half so incomprehensibly as this.

Management books (and, heaven knows, there are enough of them – some 3,000 business titles are published every year in the United States alone) can be excused for indulging in some jargon, since most of them are written for other managers. Even prize-winning books do it. "Each value stream within the operating system must be optimised individually from end to end," is a not untypical sentence from a book called *Journey to Lean*, the winner of an award in 2004 from Britain's Management Consultancies Association.

A glance along a bookshelf of management writing throws up titles such as *Deep Smarts*, which, in case you didn't guess, is "a potent form of experience-based wisdom that drives both organisational competitiveness and personal success"; and *The HR Value Proposition*, which shows how "HR creates value for internal stakeholders", without asking how painful that might be.

> **not only do businessmen write pompous rubbish, they speak it as well**

In *The Jargon of the Professions*, the book's author, Kenneth Hudson, writes that "not only do businessmen write pompous rubbish, they speak it as well". And they have been doing so for some time. He quotes a 1974 example of the chairman of a large British engineering concern who was asked in a television interview what he felt was the main problem of his company. His reply: "To generate the availability of exposure of our management."

Happily, some business writing is jargon-free, following George Orwell's advice to "never use a long word where a short one will do, and never use jargon if you can think of an everyday English equivalent". Among recent outstanding examples are Joan Magretta's *What Management Is*, and John Roberts's *The Modern Firm*.

❝ never use jargon if you can think of an everyday English equivalent ❞

The *Harvard Business Review* too is a brave and dependable beacon in the dark and continually swirling fog of business gobbledegook. Caveat lector.

Top grossing films of all time

June 2006

Movie	Year opened	Budget, $m	US box office, $m	World box office, $m	Adjusted* world box office, $m
Gone With the Wind	1939	3	199	391	1,333
Star Wars	1977	11	461	798	1,153
E.T.	1982	na	435	757	915
Titanic	1997	200	601	1,835	839
Jaws	1975	12	260	471	832
The Exorcist	1973	12	205	358	654
The Empire Strikes Back	1980	18	290	534	624
Return of the Jedi	1983	33	309	573	599
Raiders of the Lost Ark	1981	20	242	384	552
Jurassic Park	1993	63	357	920	546
Star Wars: Episode I -- The Phantom Menace	1999	110	431	926	544
Forrest Gump	1994	55	330	680	500
Close Encounters of the Third Kind	1977	na	128	300	495
The Lion King	1994	na	313	772	474
Grease	1978	6	182	380	454
Shrek 2	2004	75	437	912	451
Spider-Man	2002	139	404	807	446
Independence Day	1996	75	306	813	444
Beverly Hills Cop	1984	na	235	316	443
Home Alone	1990	na	286	534	427

*Adjusted to 2005 average ticket price.

Source: *The Movie Times* (www.the-movie-times.com)

Business laws and principles

BENFORD'S LAW In lists of numbers from many sources of data the leading digit 1 occurs much more often than the others (about 30% of the time). The law was discovered by Simon Newcomb, an American astronomer, in 1881. He noted that the first pages of books of logarithms were much more thumbed than others. Furthermore, the higher the digit, the less likely it is to occur. This applies to mathematical constants as much as utility bills, addresses, share prices, birth and death statistics, the height of mountains, etc.

BROOKS'S LAW "Adding manpower to a late software project makes it later," said Fred Brooks, in his book *The Mythical Man-Month*.

GRESHAM'S LAW "Bad money drives good money out of circulation." If coins of the same legal tender contain metal of different value, the coins composed of the cheaper metal will be used for payment, and those made of more expensive metal will be hoarded and disappear from circulation. Named after Sir Thomas Gresham (1519–79), a British financier and founder of the Royal Exchange.

MOORE'S LAW "The number of transistors on a chip doubles every 18 months." An observation by Gordon Moore, a founder of Intel, regarding the pace of semiconductor technology development in 1961.

MURPHY'S LAW Anything that can go wrong will go wrong.

PARKINSON'S LAW "Work expands so as to fill the time available for its completion" was formulated by Cecil Northcote Parkinson in *The Economist* in 1955.

PARKINSON'S LAW OF DATA Data expand to fill the space available for storage, so acquiring more memory will encourage the adoption of techniques that require more memory.

THE PETER PRINCIPLE In a hierarchy, every employee tends to rise to his level of incompetence, according to Laurence Peter and Raymond Hull in their book of the same name published in 1969.

REILLY'S LAW This law of retail gravitation suggests that people are generally attracted to the largest shopping centre in the area. William Reilly, an American academic, proposed the law in a book published in 1931.

PARETO PRINCIPLE Also known as the 80/20 rule and named after Vilfredo Pareto (1848–1923), an Italian economist, who determined that 80% of activity comes from 20% of the people. The principle was extended (or simply misunderstood) by Joseph Juran, an American management guru, who suggested that for many phenomena 80% of consequences stem from 20% of the causes. That is, in many instances a large number of results stem from a small number of causes, eg, 80% of problems come from 20% of the equipment or workforce.

SAY'S LAW Aggregate supply creates its own aggregate demand. Attributed to Jean-Baptiste Say (1767–1832), a French economist. If output increases in a free-market economy, the sales would give the producers of the goods the same amount of income which would re-enter the economy and create demand for those goods. Keynes's law, attributed to John Maynard Keynes (1883–1946), a British economist, says that the opposite is true and that "demand creates its own supply" as businesses produce more to satisfy demand up to the limit of full employment.

Top business schools

EIU ranking, 2005

University of Navarra – IESE Business School	Spain
Northwestern University – Kellogg School of Management	US
Dartmouth College – Tuck School of Business	US
Stanford Graduate School of Business	US
IMD – International Institute for Management Development	Switzerland
University of Chicago – Graduate School of Business	US
New York University – Leonard Stern School of Business	US
University of Michigan – Ross School of Business	US
Columbia Business School	US
University of California at Berkeley – Haas School of Business	US
INSEAD	France/ Singapore
Vlerick Leuven Gent Management School	Belgium
Massachusetts Institute of Technology – MIT Sloan School of Management	US

Source: Economist Intelligence Unit

FT ranking, 2006

University of Pennsylvania – Wharton School	US
Harvard Business School	US
Stanford Graduate School of Business	US
Columbia Business School	US
London Business School	UK
University of Chicago – Graduate School of Business	US
New York University – Leonard Stern School of Business	US
Dartmouth College – Tuck School of Business	US
INSEAD	France/Singapore
Massachusetts Institute of Technology – MIT Sloan School of Management	US
Yale School of Management	US
IE – Instituto de Empresa	Spain
University of Navarra – IESE Business School	Spain
IMD – International Institute for Management Development	Switzerland

Source: *Financial Times*

Business school costs and rewards

	Cost*, $'000	Five-year gain†, $'000	Pre-MBA salary, $'000	Post-MBA salary, $'000
US				
Dartmouth College – Tuck School of Business	75	134	54	165
University of Pennsylvania – Wharton School	75	129	64	177
University of Chicago – Graduate School of Business	75	121	60	164
Columbia Business School	75	120	57	160
Yale School of Management	72	119	46	134
Stanford Graduate School of Business	78	115	58	160
Harvard Business School	71	113	62	180
Outside US				
INSEAD	54	165	60	165
London Business School	76	149	46	145
IMD – International Institute for Management Development	43	141	74	161
University of Navarra – IESE Business School	59	139	32	109
SDA Bocconi	38	137	40	117
IE – Instituto de Empresa	47	133	37	100
University of Oxford – Saïd Business School	42	120	53	144
Cranfield School of Management	46	105	51	127
University of Cambridge – Judge Business School	39	104	47	127
York University – Schulich School of Business	41	104	26	89
RSM Erasmus University	41	103	40	125

†Five-year total compensation after graduation minus the sum of tuition and forgone compensation.
Note: *Out-of-state tuition for complete MBA.
Source: *Forbes*

From PCs to PDAs

Worldwide PC unit shipments by region

Region	2003	2004	2005
Asia-Pacific	24,450,096	27,914,774	31,380,848
Canada	2,434,600	2,698,500	3,116,000
Central/eastern Europe	7,128,146	8,592,836	9,837,482
Japan	6,174,239	6,402,764	6,848,501
Latin America	7,171,276	9,315,073	11,999,442
Middle East/Africa	4,059,930	5,004,240	6,091,260
US	36,959,327	39,352,166	39,697,902
Western Europe	23,131,237	25,238,776	27,134,701
Worldwide	111,508,851	124,519,128	136,106,136

Worldwide notebook and ultra portable shipments

Region	Form factor	2003	2004	2005
Worldwide	Notebook	35,426,536	43,865,481	59,412,310
Worldwide	Ultra Portable	3,938,724	5,059,138	5,888,260

Worldwide PDA Shipments

Region	2003	2004	2005
Worldwide	10,572,143	9,127,726	7,646,638

Source: IDC

Worldwide BlackBerry Shipments

Region	2003	2004	2005
Worldwide	490,263	2,660,899	4,072,122

Note: Figures for Research In Motion include only Smartphones, not its PDA shipments.
Source: IDC

Chip power

	Transistors, m	Processor
1971	0.00225	4004
1972	0.0025	8008
1974	0.005	8080
1978	0.029	8086
1982	0.12	286
1985	0.275	Intel386
1989	1.18	Intel486
1993	3.1	Pentium
1997	7.5	Pentium II
1999	28	Pentium III
2000	42	Pentium 4
2002	220	Itanium
2004	592	Itanium 2
2006	1,720	Dual-core Itanium 2

Source: Intel

Computer processing costs

Year	1944	1970	1984	1997	2006
Cost $	200,000	4,674,160	3,995	999	649
MIPS*	0.000003	12.5	8.3	166	27,100
$ per MIPS	65,941,300,000	373,933	479	6	0.02

*Millions of instructions per second.
Sources: Federal Reserve Bank of Dallas; *The Economist*

The impact of software piracy

Losses by region, 2005

	$bn
Western Europe	11.83
Asia-Pacific	8.05
US & Canada	7.69
Eastern Europe	3.08
Latin America	2.03
Middle East & Africa	1.62

Losses by country, 2005

	$bn
US	6.90
China	3.88
France	3.19
Germany	1.92
UK	1.80
Russia	1.63
Japan	1.62
Italy	1.56
Canada	0.78
Brazil	0.77
Spain	0.77
Netherlands	0.60
India	0.57
Mexico	0.53
South Korea	0.40
Poland	0.39
Switzerland	0.38
Australia	0.36
Sweden	0.34
Indonesia	0.28
Turkey	0.27
Thailand	0.26

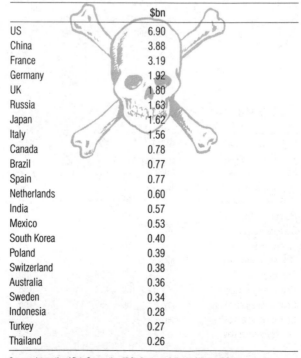

Sources: International Data Corporation (IDC); Business Software Alliance (BSA)

Spam and e-mail

Leading spam-producing countries

2005	% of total
US	24.50
China (incl. Hong Kong)	22.30
South Korea	9.70
France	5.00
Canada	3.00
Brazil	2.60
Spain	2.50
Austria	2.40
Taiwan	2.10
Poland	2.00
Japan	2.00
Germany	1.80

Source: Sophos

You have junk mail

Spam and e-mail forecasts

Bn except where specified	2006	2007	2008	2009	2010
Worldwide messages sent per day	171	196	228	267	315
Worldwide spam traffic per day	121	141	170	203	250
Spam as % of total messages per day	71	72	75	76	79
Delivered spam messages per day	70	80	96	112	135
Corporate messages per day	63	73	84	99	116
Corporate spam traffic per day	35	42	53	65	85
Corporate spam as % of corporate messages per day	56	58	63	66	73
Delivered corporate spam messages per day	23	27	33	39	50
Consumer messages per day	108	124	144	168	198
Consumer spam messages per day	86	99	117	138	165
Consumer spam as % of consumer messages per day	79	80	81	82	83

Source: The Radicati Group

Pod facts

iPod sales, m

2003	1,482,867	2005	31,960,000
2004	8,263,000	2006*	16,637,000

*First half.
Source: Apple

Legal music downloads by single tracks downloaded, m

	2004	2005	Growth, %
Europe	14	62	355
US	143	353	147
World	156	419	169

Source: IFPI

Worldwide portable digital music player shipments, m

	2001	2002	2003	2004	2005	2006*
Flash	2.1	2.8	12.5	26.4	101.5	149.8
Hard-drive	0.4	0.9	2.7	12.5	20.5	21.5
Total	2.4	3.7	15.1	38.9	122.0	171.4

*Forecast.
Source: IDC

Podcast growth

	FeedBurner-managed podcasts and videocast feeds, '000	Feed subscribers, m
Jan 2005	1.671	0.221
Jan 2006	35.132	8.400
Jul 2006	59.724	19.182

Source: FeedBurner

The podcasting world

	Number of Feedburner-managed podcasts, May 2006	% of world total
US	446,038	61.4
UK	46,110	6.3
Canada	34,303	4.7
Japan	32,405	4.5
Germany	27,157	3.7
France	19,515	2.7
Australia	15,372	2.1
Italy	7,636	1.1
Spain	7,492	1.0
Other	90,694	12.5
World total	726,722	100.0

Source: FeedBurner

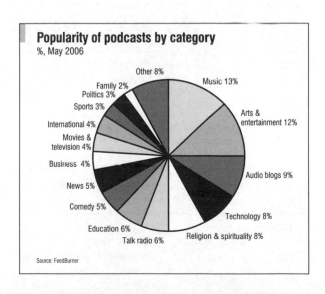

Popularity of podcasts by category
%, May 2006

Other 8%
Family 2%
Politics 3%
Sports 3%
International 4%
Movies & television 4%
Business 4%
News 5%
Comedy 5%
Education 6%
Talk radio 6%
Religion & spirituality 8%
Technology 8%
Audio blogs 9%
Arts & entertainment 12%
Music 13%

Source: FeedBurner

Internet suffixes

Afghanistan	.af	Burkina Faso	.bf
Albania	.al	Burundi	.bi
Algeria	.dz	Cambodia	.kh
American Samoa	.as	Cameroon	.cm
Andorra	.ad	Canada	.ca
Angola	.ao	Cape Verde	.cv
Anguilla	.ai	Cayman Islands	.ky
Antarctica	.aq	Central African Rep.	.cf
Antigua & Barbuda	.ag	Chad	.td
Argentina	.ar	Chile	.cl
Armenia	.am	China	.cn
Aruba	.aw	Christmas Island	.cx
Ascension Island	.ac	Cocos (Keeling) Islands	.cc
Australia	.au	Colombia	.co
Austria	.at	Comoros	.km
Azerbaijan	.az	Congo (Democratic	
Bahamas	.bs	Republic of Congo)	.cd
Bahrain	.bh	Congo-Brazzaville	
Bangladesh	.bd	(Republic of Congo)	.cg
Barbados	.bb	Cook Islands	.ck
Belarus	.by	Costa Rica	.cr
Belgium	.be	Côte d'Ivoire	.ci
Belize	.bz	Croatia	.hr
Benin	.bj	Cuba	.cu
Bermuda	.bm	Cyprus	.cy
Bhutan	.bt	Czech Republic	.cz
Bolivia	.bo	Denmark	.dk
Bosnia	.ba	Djibouti	.dj
Botswana	.bw	Dominica	.dm
Bouvet Island	.bv	Dominican Republic	.do
Brazil	.br	East Timor	.tp
British Indian Ocean		Ecuador	.ec
Territory	.io	Egypt	.eg
Brunei	.bn	El Salvador	.sv
Bulgaria	.bg	Equatorial Guinea	.gq

Eritrea	.er	Iraq	.iq
Estonia	.ee	Ireland	.ie
Ethiopia	.et	Isle of Man	.im
Falkland Islands	.fk	Israel	.il
Faroe Islands	.fo	Italy	.it
Fiji	.fj	Jamaica	.jm
Finland	.fi	Japan	.jp
France	.fr	Jersey	.je
French Guyana	.gf	Jordan	.jo
French Polynesia	.pf	Kazakhstan	.kz
French Southern		Kenya	.ke
Territories	.tf	Kyrgyzstan	.kg
Gabon	.ga	Kiribati	.ki
Gambia, The	.gm	Kuwait	.kw
Georgia	.ge	Laos	.la
Germany	.de	Latvia	.lv
Ghana	.gh	Lebanon	.lb
Gibraltar	.gi	Lesotho	.ls
Greece	.gr	Liberia	.lr
Greenland	.gl	Libya	.ly
Grenada	.gd	Liechtenstein	.li
Guadeloupe	.gp	Lithuania	.lt
Guam	.gu	Luxembourg	.lu
Guatemala	.gt	Macau	.mo
Guernsey	.gg	Macedonia	.mk
Guinea	.gn	Madagascar	.mg
Guinea-Bissau	.gw	Malawi	.mw
Guyana	.gy	Malaysia	.my
Haiti	.ht	Maldives	.mv
Heard & McDonald		Mali	.ml
Islands	.hm	Malta	.mt
Honduras	.hn	Marshall Islands	.mh
Hong Kong	.hk	Martinique	.mq
Hungary	.hu	Mauritania	.mr
Iceland	.is	Mauritius	.mu
India	.in	Mayotte	.yt
Indonesia	.id	Mexico	.mx
Iran	.ir	Micronesia	.fm

internet suffixes *continued*

Moldova	.md	Puerto Rico	.pr
Monaco	.mc	Qatar	.qa
Mongolia	.mn	Réunion	.re
Monserrat	.ms	Romania	.ro
Morocco	.ma	Russia	.ru
Mozambique	.mz	Rwanda	.rw
Myanmar	.mm	St Helena	.sh
Namibia	.na	St Kitts & Nevis	.kn
Nauru	.nr	St Lucia	.lc
Nepal	.np	St Pierre & Miquelon	.pm
Netherlands	.nl	St Vincent &	
Netherlands Antilles	.an	the Grenadines	.vc
New Caledonia	.nc	Samoa	.ws
New Zealand	.nz	San Marino	.sm
Nicaragua	.ni	São Tomé & Príncipe	.st
Niger	.ne	Saudi Arabia	.sa
Nigeria	.ng	Senegal	.sn
Niue	.nu	Seychelles	.sc
Norfolk Island	.nf	Serbia & Montenegro	.yu
North Korea (Democratic		Sierra Leone	.sl
People's Republic		Singapore	.sg
of Korea)	.kp	Slovakia	.sk
Northern Mariana		Slovenia	.si
Islands	.mp	Solomon Islands	.sb
Norway	.no	Somalia	.so
Oman	.om	South Africa	.za
Pakistan	.pk	South Korea	
Palau	.pw	(Republic of Korea)	.kr
Palestinian Territories	.ps	South Georgia & the	
Panama	.pa	South Sandwich	
Papua New Guinea	.pg	Islands	.gs
Paraguay	.py	Spain	.es
Peru	.pe	Sri Lanka	.lk
Philippines	.ph	Sudan	.sd
Pitcairn	.pn	Suriname	.sr
Poland	.pl	Svalbard &	
Portugal	.pt	Jan Mayen Islands	.sj

Swaziland	.sz	Aviation	.aero	
Sweden	.se	Business		
Switzerland	.ch	organisations	.biz	
Syria	.sy	Commercial	.com	
Taiwan	.tw	Co-operative		
Tajikistan	.tj	organisations	.coop	
Tanzania	.tz	Educational	.edu	
Thailand	.th	US government	.gov	
Togo	.tg	Open TLD		
Tokelau	.tk	(Top level domain)	.info	
Tonga	.to	International		
Trinidad & Tobago	.tt	organisations	.int	
Tunisia	.tn	US Department of		
Turkey	.tr	Defence	.mil	
Turkmenistan	.tm	Museums	.museum	
Turks & Caicos Islands	.tc	Personal	.name	
Tuvalu	.tv	Networks	.net	
Uganda	.ug	Organisations	.org	
Ukraine	.ua			
United Arab Emirates	.ae			
United Kingdom	.uk			
United States	.us			
United States Minor Outlying Islands	.um			
Uruguay	.uy			
Uzbekistan	.uz			
Vanuatu	.vu			
Vatican	.va			
Venezuela	.ve			
Vietnam	.vn			
Virgin Islands, British	.vg			
Virgin Islands, US	.vi			
Wallis & Futuna Islands	.wf			
Western Sahara	.eh			
Yemen	.ye			
Zaire	.cd			
Zambia	.zm			
Zimbabwe	.zw			

Internet suffixes

Source: Internet Assigned Numbers Authority

Internet usage

World internet usage, March 2006

Region	Internet users, m	Penetration, %	% of world usage	Usage growth, 2000–05, %
Africa	23.6	2.6	2.3	423.9
Asia	364.3	9.9	35.6	218.7
Europe	291.6	36.1	28.5	177.5
Middle East	18.2	9.6	1.8	454.2
North America	227.3	68.6	22.2	110.3
Latin America & Caribbean	80.0	14.4	7.8	342.5
Oceania/ Australia	17.9	52.6	1.7	134.6
World total	1,022.9	15.7	100.0	183.4

Source: internetworldstats.com

Top ten languages, March 2006

Language	Internet users, m	% of all users	Speakers, m	Penetration, %	Growth in users, 2000–05, %
English	312.8	30.6	1,125.7	27.8	128.0
Chinese	132.3	13.0	1,340.7	9.9	309.6
Japanese	86.3	8.5	128.4	67.2	83.3
Spanish	80.6	7.9	429.3	18.8	229.2
German	56.9	5.6	96.0	59.2	106.0
French	41.0	4.0	381.2	10.7	235.9
Korean	33.9	3.3	73.9	45.8	78.0
Portuguese	32.4	3.2	230.8	14.0	327.3
Italian	28.9	2.8	59.1	48.8	118.7
Russian	23.7	2.3	143.7	16.5	664.5
Other	194.2	19.0	2,490.8	7.8	421.6
World total	1,022.9	100.0	6,499.7	15.7	183.4

Source: internwetworldstats.com

Global average internet usage, May 2006

Sessions/visits per person per month	34
Domains visited per person per month	70
Web pages per person per month	1,415
Page views per surfing session	41
PC time spent per month	29:11:24
Time spent during surfing session	00:51:31
Duration of a web page viewed	00:00:43
Active digital media universe	318,691,682
Current digital media universe estimate	475,021,461

Source: Nielsen//NetRatings

Number of internet searches performed by search engine, March 2006

Search engine	Per day, m	Per month, m
Google	91	2,733
Yahoo!	60	1,792
Microsoft MSN	28	845
AOL	16	486
Ask	13	378
Others	6	166
Total	213	6,400

Source: SearchEngineWatch

Top internet-search sites by search* market share, % of total

	Google†	Yahoo!	Microsoft MSN	Ask
Mar 2005	45.3	30.6	16.5	5.5
Mar 2006	50.3	28.0	13.2	5.9

*US-initiated.
†Includes AOL.
Source: comScore Networks

Internet growth

End year	Users, m	% of world population
1995	16.0	0.4
1996	36.0	0.9
1997	70.0	1.7
1998	159.0	2.9
1999	248.0	4.1
2000	451.0	7.4
2001	535.5	8.6
2002	597.5	9.6
2003	719.0	11.1
2004	817.0	12.7
2005	1,018.0	15.7

Source: internetworldstats.com

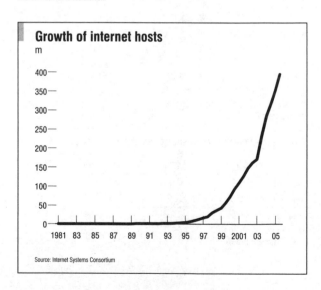

Growth of internet hosts

Source: Internet Systems Consortium

Blogs ᴀᵂᴀʸ

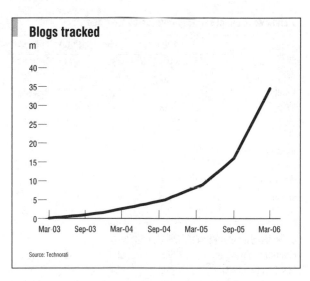

Blogs tracked
m

Source: Technorati

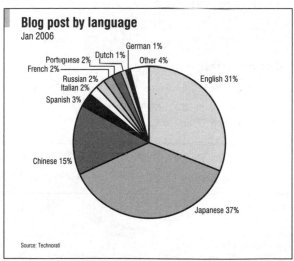

Blog post by language
Jan 2006

- German 1%
- Dutch 1%
- Portuguese 2%
- French 2%
- Russian 2%
- Italian 2%
- Spanish 3%
- Chinese 15%
- Other 4%
- English 31%
- Japanese 37%

Source: Technorati

Telephony

Worldwide telecom services revenue by type, $bn

	1991	1995	2000	2004
Fixed-line	331	428	477	552
International	37	53	60	32
Mobile	19	78	278	454
Other	53	89	165	210
Total	440	648	980	1,248
As % of total				
Fixed-line	75.2	66.0	48.7	44.2
International	8.4	8.2	6.1	2.6
Mobile	4.3	12.0	28.4	36.4
Other	12.0	13.7	16.8	16.8
Other telecom statistics				
Fixed-line subscribers, m	546	689	983	1,207
Mobile subscribers, m	16	91	740	1,758
International traffic minutes, bn	38	63	118	145
Personal computers, m	130	235	500	775

Source: International Telecommunication Union

Telephone-call prices

Cost of a three-minute call from New York to London, 1990 dollars

1930	1960	1990	1999	2006
245	47.5	3.00	0.35	0.19

Fixed-line subscribers by region, m

	2000	2005	2005 penetration, %
Africa	19.7	28.3	3.2
Americas	290.1	296.8	34.0
Asia	339.9	596.9	15.8
Europe	316.9	328.6	41.0
Oceania	12.6	13.6	42.4
World total	979.2	1,264.1	19.8

Source: International Telecommunication Union

Mobile phone subscribers by region, m

	2000	2005	2005 penetration, %
Africa	15.6	130.3	11.3
Americas	182.0	458.8	51.1
Asia	240.6	849.8	22.2
Europe	291.5	675.6	84.4
Oceania	10.3	22.5	68.5
World total	740.0	2,137.0	31.9

Source: International Telecommunication Union

The corporate high life

Aircraft ownership by Fortune 500 companies

2006	No.	%
Light jets	10	0.7%
Medium jets	690	47.8%
Heavy jets	519	36.0%
Twin-turbine helicopters	97	6.7%
Single-turbine helicopters	47	3.3%
Light turboprops	72	5.0%
Heavy turboprops	8	0.6%
Total aircraft	1,443	

Worldwide business fleets

2006	World total	North America	Europe	Asia & Middle East	Oceania	Other
Jets	14,101	10,524	1,637	494	96	1,350
Turboprops	10,551	7,166	914	394	211	1,866

Average age of worldwide business aicraft

2006	Years
Heavy jet	14.46
Medium jet	17.05
Light jet	17.08
Heavy turboprop	35.01
Medium turboprop	22.91
Light turboprop	7.97

Source: AvDataInc

Air miles to go

	Total awarded, cumulative, bn	Total unredeemed, cumulative, bn
1981	4.1	2.2
1982	20.9	6.1
1983	59.2	15.8
1984	124.3	39.0
1985	218.6	76.0
1986	342.4	127.0
1987	505.4	208.7
1988	787.5	400.0
1989	1,125.1	617.2
1990	1,519.2	877.9
1991	1,962.5	1,165.9
1992	2,461.3	1,486.1
1993	3,044.3	1,867.1
1994	3,688.3	2,232.4
1995	4,349.3	2,608.6
1996	5,179.3	3,183.3
1997	6,159.3	3,891.5
1998	7,279.3	4,608.5
1999	8,569.3	5,539.7
2000	10,009.3	6,630.2
2001	11,609.3	7,888.6
2002	13,255.3	9,131.7
2003	14,985.9	10,893.9
2004	17,226.0	12,367.3
2005	19,940.1	14,201.2

Source: WebFlyer

Vehicle production

World motor vehicle production by country and region, m

	2004	2005	% change
Europe	**20.835**	**20.801**	**0**
EU-25	18.331	18.177	-1
EU-15	16.851	16.440	-2
Austria	0.249	0.253	2
Belgium	0.900	0.929	3
Czech Republic	0.448	0.605	35
Finland	0.011	0.022	100
France	3.666	3.549	-3
Germany	5.570	5.758	3
Hungary	0.123	0.152	24
Italy	1.142	1.038	-9
Netherlands	0.248	0.181	-27
Poland	0.601	0.625	4
Portugal	0.227	0.219	-3
Romania	0.122	0.195	59
Serbia	0.015	0.014	-7
Slovakia	0.224	0.218	-2
Slovenia	0.132	0.178	35
Spain	3.012	2.753	-9
Sweden	0.340	0.339	0
Turkey	0.823	0.879	7
UK	1.857	1.803	-3
CIS	**1.543**	**1.537**	**0**
Russia	1.386	1.351	-3
Belarus	0.020	0.023	15
Ukraine	0.187	0.216	15
Uzbekistan*	0.081	0.096	19

NAFTA	**16.278**	**16.340**	**0**
Canada	2.712	2.688	-1
Mexico	1.577	1.670	6
US	11.990	11.981	0
South America	**2.669**	**2.985**	**12**
Argentina	0.260	0.320	23
Brazil	2.317	2.528	9
Chile*	0.007	0.007	-7
Colombia*	0.043	0.055	29
Ecuador*	0.004	0.025	603
Venezuela*	0.038	0.049	30
Asia-Oceania	**24.292**	**25.817**	**6**
Australia	0.411	0.395	-4
China	5.234	5.708	9
India	1.511	1.627	8
Indonesia	0.408	0.495	21
Iran	0.789	0.817	4
Japan	10.512	10.799	3
Malaysia	0.472	0.564	19
Pakistan*	0.093	0.156	68
Philippines*	0.071	0.054	-36
South Korea	3.469	3.699	7
Taiwan	0.431	0.446	4
Thailand	0.928	1.125	21
Vietnam	0.020	0.032	59
Africa	**0.423**	**0.522**	**24**
Egypt	0.049	0.069	40
Morocco*	0.013	0.015	15
South Africa	0.456	0.525	15
Total countries shown	**64.496**	**66.465**	**3**

*Estimates.

Source: International Organization of Motor Vehicle Manufacturers

vehicle production *continued*

World motor vehicle production by manufacturer, 2005, m

	Total	Passenger cars	Light commercial vehicles	Heavy trucks	Buses and coaches
General Motors	9.098	5.657	3.383	0.047	0.011
Toyota	7.338	6.157	0.943	0.186	0.052
Ford	6.497	3.514	2.904	0.079	–
Volkswagen	5.211	4.979	0.194	0.033	0.005
DaimlerChrysler	4.816	1.965	2.354	0.436	0.061
Nissan	3.494	2.697	0.651	0.140	0.006
Honda	3.436	3.324	0.049	0.063	–
PSA Peugeot-Citroën	3.375	2.983	0.393	–	–
Hyundai-Kia	3.091	2.727	0.127	0.138	0.100
Renault-Dacia-Samsung	2.617	2.195	0.422	–	–
Suzuki-Maruti	2.072	1.723	0.349	–	–
Fiat-Iveco-Irisbus	2.038	1.540	0.395	0.082	0.022
Mitsubishi	1.331	0.998	0.329	0.004	–
BMW	1.323	1.323	–	–	–
Mazda	1.288	1.091	0.193	0.002	–
Daihatsu	1.011	0.803	0.195	0.013	–
Avtovaz	0.721	0.721	–	–	–
Donfeng	0.593	–	0.403	0.180	0.010
Fuji (Subaru)	0.592	0.508	0.084	–	–
Beijing AIG	0.559	–	0.559	–	–
Other	5.964	0.951	2.731	1.065	0.071
Total	66.465*	45.856	16.658	2.468	0.338

*Includes 1.147m not included in subcategory totals.

Source: International Organization of Motor Vehicle Manufacturers

The price of petrol

Pump prices 2005, $ per US gallon

	Price excluding tax	Tax	Total
Turkey	1.83	4.91	6.74
Norway	2.25	4.00	6.25
UK	1.97	4.07	6.04
Germany	2.12	3.89	6.01
Italy	2.22	3.61	5.83
France	2.12	3.53	5.65
South Korea	1.94	3.27	5.21
Poland	2.19	2.73	4.91
Japan	2.12	2.33	4.45
Finland	1.49	2.55	4.04
Lithuania	2.07	1.90	3.98
Australia	2.12	1.56	3.68
India	1.80	1.85	3.65
Ecuador	2.15	1.46	3.61
Brazil	2.12	1.00	3.12
Canada	1.77	0.99	2.76
South Africa	1.87	0.83	2.70
US	2.04	0.46	2.50
Ghana	2.12	0.30	2.42
Jamaica	1.91	0.48	2.39
Mexico	1.71	0.49	2.20
Argentina	1.09	1.04	2.13
Guatemala	1.05	0.63	1.68
China	1.19	0.45	1.64
Russia	0.82	0.70	1.52
Saudi Arabia	0.91	0.00	0.91
Indonesia	0.57	0.09	0.66
Venezeula	0.33	0.19	0.52

1 gallon = 4.546 litres.
Source: IMF

Pedal p🅾wer

Worldwide bicycle production was 11m in 1950, 20m in 1960, 36m in 1970, 62m in 1980, 91m in 1990 and 104m in 2002. The high point was in 1988, when 105m units were produced.

China is the largest producer, with 63m bikes in 2002, 23% more than in 2001 and 61% of the world total, and 73m estimated for 2003. China's production has climbed from 42.7m in 1999 and 52.2m in 2000, with a dip to 51.2m in 2001.

As Chinese production has risen, other large producers – Japan, Taiwan and the United States – have experienced a decline. Production in Taiwan fell from 8.4m units in 1999 (7.8m exported) to 4.4 in 2002 (4.2m exported); in America from 1.7m in 1999 to 0.41m in 2002; and in Japan from 5.6m in 1999 to 3.08m in 2002.

Around 46m of China's 2002 total of 63m was exported (up from 22.7m in 1999), with the United States the largest customer, taking 18.6m units (from an import total of 19.3m).

Vietnam was the fastest-growing producer in 2002, producing 2m units, a 250% increase compared with 2001.

Estimates of the number of bikes in Beijing, China's capital, range from 4m to 10m, and in 2004, the 4-yuan annual tax on bikes was dropped. However, as car numbers increase by 20,000 per month, bike journeys are estimated to have dropped by 60% in ten years.

By 2005, 1,250 former rail corridors in the United States had been converted to cycle trails (a total of 12,650 miles). In 2004 the total was 1,212 (12,585 miles) and in 1988 it was 198 (359 miles).

Health-care providers in Africa are increasingly using bicycles, especially for delivery of immunisation programmes. Two projects in Senegal reported a 58% increase in speed by nurses using cycles on their rounds rather than walking, and a saving of 40c per journey compared with those using taxis.

Another scheme is tackling Africa's conflict problems – in the Democratic Republic of the Congo, an NGO-run programme in the troubled Katanga region under which guns could be exchanged for bicycles proved highly successful: by July 2006, around 6,500 weapons had been turned in and destroyed.

Germany and the Netherlands lead the way in cycle-friendly safety measures, such as cycle paths, traffic calming and urban design. Cyclists in America are twice as likely to be killed as those in Germany, and more than three times as likely as cyclists in the Netherlands.

Cyclist deaths in America have fallen over the past 25 years, but only because numbers of cyclists – particularly children – have dropped. The percentage of children walking or cycling to school has dropped from 71% to 18% over a generation.

British government tax measures to promote cycling include the ability to claim tax relief of up to 20p per mile cycled in the course of business – excluding travel to and from work.

In London in 2006, cycle journeys had increased by 72% over 2000 (100% in summer months), to 3.15m journeys per week – still only 2% of total journeys, compared to 28% in Amsterdam. Bikes are owned by 51% of Londoners.

In the Netherlands, a population of just over 16m is estimated to own 17m bikes, with 3.4m daily commutes being made by bike. Bicycle theft in Amsterdam is estimated at around 180,000 per year.

Sources: World Watch Institute; *Bicycle Retailer and Industry News*; *Guardian*; *Time Out London*; BBC

Ship ahoy

Merchant fleets

2004 By country of registration, gross tonnage		By country of ownership, gross tonnage, m	
Panama	141.8	Greece	95.6
Liberia	59.6	Japan	89.3
Bahamas	38.4	Germany	54.4
Singapore	30.9	China	41.5
Greece	30.7	US	36.0
Hong Kong	29.8	Norway	33.4
Malta	23.0	Hong Kong	26.4
China	22.3	UK	22.1
Cyprus	19.0	South Korea	19.3
Norway	14.2	Taiwan	16.1
Japan	12.8	Denmark	15.2
Italy	11.6	Singapore	14.3
Germany	11.5	Russia	13.0
UK	11.2	Italy	12.2
US	11.1	Switzerland	9.6

Source: Lloyd's Register

Runway popularity

Total passengers, m

Atlanta, Hartsfield	85.9	Denver, Intl.	43.3
Chicago, O'Hare	76.5	Madrid, Barajas Intl.	41.9
London, Heathrow	67.9	Memphis, Intl.	3.6
Tokyo, Haneda	63.3	Hong Kong, Intl.	3.4
Los Angeles, Intl.	61.5	Anchorage, Intl.	2.6
Dallas, Ft. Worth	59.1	Tokyo, Narita	2.3
Paris, Charles de Gaulle	53.8	Seoul, Inchon	2.2
Frankfurt, Main	52.2	Frankfurt, Main	2.0
Las Vegas, McCarran Intl.	44.3	Los Angeles, Intl.	1.9
Amsterdam, Schipol	44.2	Shanghai, Pudong Intl.	1.9

Source: Airports Council International

Inventors and inventions

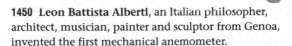

1450 Leon Battista Alberti, an Italian philosopher, architect, musician, painter and sculptor from Genoa, invented the first mechanical anemometer.

1756 John Smeaton, a British engineer, made concrete by adding aggregate to cement. In 1824, Joseph Aspdin, another Briton, invented Portland cement by burning ground limestone and clay together. In 1867, Joseph Monier, a French gardener, patented the idea of reinforced concrete.

1830 Edwin Beard Budding, an engineer from Stroud in Gloucestershire, was awarded the first patent for a mechanical lawn mower.

1843 Alexander Bain, a Scottish clockmaker, patented the fax machine – 33 years before a patent was granted for the telephone. The first commercial fax service was opened between Paris and Lyon in 1865.

1849 Walter Hunt, a New York inventor, received a patent for the safety pin.

1851 Elias Howe patented an Automatic Continuous Clothing Closure but took the invention no further. In 1896, Whitcomb Judson marketed the Clasp Locker, a hook-and-eye shoe fastener. In 1913, Gideon Sundback, a Swedish-born electrical engineer living in Canada, improved the Judson C-curity Fastener and came up with the modern zip.

1861 Elisha Otis patented the "Improvement in Hoisting Apparatus". Lifts had been in use for some time but Otis invented a safety mechanism that stopped the lift falling if the rope broke, thus opening the way for safe passenger lifts and allowing the development of the high-rise building.

inventors and inventions *continued*

1866 **George McGill** developed the Patent Single Stroke Staple Press to insert brass fasteners into papers. In 1895 the Jones Manufacturing Company of Norwalk, Connecticut, introduced the first stapler that used steel staples formed into a continuous strip.

1872 **Aaron Montgomery Ward** sent out the world's first mail-order catalogue for his Chicago-based business.

1873 **Joseph Glidden**, a farmer from De Kalb, Illinois, applied for a patent on barbed wire.

1873 **Levi Strauss**, a Bavarian immigrant who had travelled to California during the Gold Rush, and Jacob Davis, a tailor from Reno, Nevada, got a patent for trousers strengthened with rivets to make sturdy workwear. Soon after they began to produce the first blue denim jeans.

1876 **Alexander Graham Bell** unveiled his "electrical speech machine" in Boston, Massachusetts, later to become known as the telephone, making the first ever

> **the first ever phone call was 'Mr Watson, come here, I want you'**

phone call to his assistant: "Mr Watson, come here, I want you." He filed for a patent on the invention hours before a competitor, Elisha Grey. Though neither had produced a working telephone at the time, Bell's device controversially incorporated elements of his competitor's phone that had not appeared in his original patent.

1877 **Thomas Edison** invented the tin-foil phonograph. Alexander Graham Bell's graphophone of 1883 employed a wax cylinder which could be played many times but required separate sound recording for each cylinder. In 1887, Emile Berliner, a German immigrant working in

Washington, DC, was granted a patent for the gramophone on which multiple, reproducable, pre-recorded flat-disc records could be played.

1879 Thomas Edison invented the first practical electric light bulb. Though the idea was not new no one had previously managed to produce a bulb that was cheap and robust enough for mass production.

1883 James Ritty and John Birch got a patent for the first mechanical cash register, invented for use in Ritty's saloon in Dayton, Ohio.

1888 Marvin Stone of Washington, DC, patented a spiral-winding process to manufacture the first wax-coated paper drinking straws.

1888 Thomas Edison filed a patent for the Kinetoscope, the forerunner of the modern motion-picture camera.

1891 James Naismith, a Canadian physical-education instructor, invented basketball.

1895 Charles Fey, a San Francisco car mechanic, invented the first mechanical fruit machine, the Liberty Bell.

1895 Guglielmo Marconi sent wireless signals over a mile at his laboratory in Italy. The next year, in Britain, he was granted the world's first patent for a system of wireless telegraphy.

1899 Johan Vaaler, a Norwegian inventor, was granted a patent for the paperclip in Germany. His design never really caught on as the Gem paperclip (the type most common today) was already in production in Britain.

1903 Albert Parkhouse, an employee of Timberlake Wire and Novelty Company in Jackson, Michigan, invented a coat hanger made from a piece of bent wire with the ends twisted together to form a hook. Colleagues had apparently complained that the firm provided insufficient coat storage.

inventors and inventions *continued*

1908 **Jacques Brandenberger**, a Swiss engineer working for a French textile company, invented Cellophane.

1921 **Earle Dickson**, a cotton-buyer at Johnson & Johnson, invented the Band-Aid self-adhesive plaster.

1921 **John Larson**, a medical student at the University of California, invented the polygraph, a lie-detecting machine.

1927 **Erik Rotheim**, a Norwegian, patented the first aerosol can that dispensed products using a propellant system.

1930 **Scotch tape**, the world's first transparent cellophane adhesive tape, was introduced. It was invented by Richard Drew, an engineer at 3M, a company located in St Paul, Minnesota. John Borden, another 3M engineer, invented the tape dispenser with a built-in cutter in 1932.

1932 **Carlton Cole Magee** invented the first parking meter in response to the growing problem of parking congestion in Oklahoma City. They were first installed there three years later.

1934 **Percy Shaw**, a 23-year-old British inventor, patented cats eyes to assist driving in fog or at night.

1938 **Laszlo Biro**, a Hungarian journalist, invented the ballpoint pen.

1938 **Polytetrafluoroethylene** (or PTFE) was discovered by Roy Plunkett at DuPont's research facility in New Jersey. PTFE was first marketed as Teflon in 1945.

1940 **Norman Breakey** of Toronto invented the paint roller.

1942 **Cyanoacrylate** was invented by Harry Coover at the Kodak Research Laboratories while developing a plastic for gunsights. The product was not considered for commercial application until 1958 and later became known as superglue.

1947 The transistor was invented at Bell Telephone Laboratories by a team led by physicists John Bardeen, Walter Brattain and William Shockley. In 1958, Jack Kilby of Texas Instruments unveiled the integrated circuit, but in 1959 Fairchild Semiconductor filed a patent for a semiconductor integrated circuit invented by Robert Noyce, starting a ten-year legal battle over who had invented the chip. In 1968, Ted Hoff, an employee of Intel, invented the microprocessor. In 1970, Doug Engelbart received a patent for his "X-Y position indicator for a display system", which was developed into the computer mouse. In 1976, Steve Jobs and Steve Wozniak made a microprocessor computer board called Apple I and a year after introduced the Apple II, the world's first personal computer.

> **❝...starting a ten-year battle over who had invented the chip❞**

1951 George de Mestral patented Velcro. The Swiss engineer, a keen mountaineer and inventor, noticed how burrs attached themselves to his clothes and his dog's fur and developed the idea for his new fastener.

1952 Joseph Woodland and Bernard Silver, graduate students at the Drexel Institute of Technology in Philadelphia, were issued a patent for the forerunner of the bar code.

1953 Norm Larsen, a chemist, made many attempts to develop an anti-corrosion formula working on the principle of water displacement in his lab in San Diego, California. In 1953, he succeeded and WD-40 (standing for water displacement 40th attempt) was born.

1954 Dee Horton and Lew Hewitt invented the automatic sliding door in Corpus Christi, Texas. The first door that entered service in 1960 was a unit donated to the City of Corpus Christi.

1955 Eugene Polley, an engineer working for America's Zenith Corporation, created the Flash-matic, the first wireless television remote control.

1956 Christopher Cockerell, a British engineer, invented the hovercraft.

1956 Bette Nesmith Graham, a secretary in Dallas, Texas, sold the first batch of Mistake Out, a liquid correcting fluid. Some years later, the product much improved, it was renamed Liquid Paper.

1958 Alfred Neustadter from Brooklyn, New York, first marketed the Rolodex, a rotating index-card holder.

1959 Ernie Fraze invented the easy-open ring-pull can in Kettering, Ohio, reputedly after struggling to open a can of beer at a family picnic.

1965 James Russell was granted 22 patents relating to his compact-disk system. CDs only came into wide use after they were taken up by Philips, a Dutch electronics firm, in 1980.

1965 James Faria and Robert Wright of Monsanto Industries filed a patent for a monofilament ribbon surface that would later become Astro Turf.

1968 Spencer Silver, a researcher at 3M looking into improving adhesives, came up with a new glue that produced a very weak bond. Art Fry, another researcher, who had often become frustrated when bookmarks fell out of his hymnal in church, eventually came up with a use for the product. Post-it notes were introduced in 1980.

1968 Roy Jacuzzi invented the first self-contained whirlpool bath with built-in water jets.

1979 Gordon Matthews's firm VMX (Voice Message Express) in Dallas, Texas, applied for a patent for the first voicemail system, which he then sold to 3M.

1981 IBM launched the first personal computer complete with a new operating system developed by a fledgling software company, the "Microsoft disk operating system" or MS-DOS.

1983 Microsoft announced that its new operating system would be on sale by the next year. Though originally called Interface Manager, the product was soon renamed Windows.

1988 Bryan Molloy and Klaus Schmiegel invented a class of aryloxyphenylpropylamines which included fluoxetine hydrochloride. It was the active ingredient in Eli Lilly's new drug, Prozac, the world's most widely used antidepressant.

❝Prozac, the world's most widely used antidepressant❞

1989 Tim Berners-Lee, a British scientist at CERN, a particle physics laboratory in Switzerland, developed a system to ease the sharing of databases and information. In 1990, he created the hypertext transfer protocol (HTTP) to allow computers to communicate over the internet. He also designed the Uniform Resource Locator (URL) to give sites addresses on the internet and invented a browser program to retrieve hypertext documents called the world wide web (WWW).

Famous patents

Invention	Year patented	Who by
Cotton gin	1794	Eli Whitney
Rubber vulcanisation	1844	Charles Goodyear
Manner of buoying vessels	1849	Abraham Lincoln
Elevator brake	1861	Elisha Graves Otis
Cast steel plough	1865	John Deere
Typewriter	1868	Christopher Sholes
Telephone/telegraphy	1876	Alexander Graham Bell
Statue of Liberty	1879	Auguste Bartholdi
Electric light	1880	Thomas Alva Edison
Electric light	1881	Lewis Howard Latimer
Punch-card tabulator	1889	Herman Hollerith
Radio	1897	Guglielmo Marconi
Internal-combustion engine	1898	Rudolf Diesel
Aspirin	1900	Felix Hoffmann
Electric railway	1901	Granville T Woods
Air conditioner	1906	Willis Haviland Carrier
Flying machine	1906	Orville and Wilbur Wright
Automobile	1911	Henry Ford
X-ray tube	1916	William D. Coolidge
Diving suit	1921	Harry Houdini
Traffic signal	1923	Garrett A. Morgan
Paint and stain/process of producing same	1925	George Washington Carver
Climbing rose (first plant patented)	1931	Henry F. Bosenberg
Electrophotography (Xerox)	1939	Chester F. Carlson
Flourescent lamp	1939	Edmund Germer
Polyurethane	1942	William E. Hanford/ Donald F. Holmes
Television receiver	1948	Louis W. Parker
Transistor	1950	John Bardeen/Walter H. Brattain/William B. Shockley

Invention	Year patented	Who by
Oral contraceptive	1954	Frank B. Colton
Nuclear fission	1955	Enrico Fermi
Pulse transfer controlling devices (magnetic core memory forerunner)	1955	An Wang
Video tape recording	1955	Charles P. Ginsburg
Random Access Memory (RAM)	1956	Jay W. Forrester
Polypropylene plastics	1958	Robert Banks/Paul Hogan
Laser	1960	Arthur Shawlow/Charles Townes
Safety belt	1962	Nils I. Bohlin
Computer mouse	1970	Douglas Engelbert
Optical fibres	1972	Donald Keck/Robert Maurer/Peter Schultz
Knee implant prosthesis	1975	Ysidro M. Martinez
Personal computer	1979	Steve Wozniak
Genetic engineering	1980	Herb Boyer/Stan Cohen
Prozac	1982	Bryan B. Molloy/Klaus Schmiegel
Transgenic non-human mammals (first animal patent – "The mouse that went to Harvard")	1988	Philip Leder

Sources: United States Patent and Trademarks Office; National Inventors' Hall of Fame

Business etiquette tips

Business cards

In Asia and East Asia, the giving and receiving of business cards is a formal affair. Offer your card with both hands, and accept graciously those you are handed (do not shove them into a pocket).

In Japan, have a business card (a *meishi*) with you at all times. Failure to offer one signals that you are not interested in pursuing the relationship.

When visiting China or Japan, have your business cards printed in English on one side and Chinese or Japanese on the other. Cards should be presented with the Japanese or Chinese side facing up.

In India, it is usual to include academic qualifications on business cards.

Names and titles and status

In Japan, although things are changing, be cautious about calling people by their first name; first names are often restricted to family and very close friends. In general, it's best to couple someone's last name with "san" (for example, Koizumi-*san*); this works for both men and women.

Chinese names appear in a different order to those in the West. The family name is followed by the generational name and then a given name. The generational and given names are usually separted by a hyphen. Some Chinese people use the initials of their generational and given names, hence Lee Cheng-kwan can be

> **many people adopt an English first name or nickname**

known as C K Lee or Mr Lee. However, many people adopt an English first name or nickname to make it easier for westerners to address them. Some of these adopted names are a little odd – so don't be surprised if you run into Ivan Ho in Hong Kong.

Germans like to be called by titles, such as doctor or professor, and will prove much friendlier if you appear to appreciate their educational credentials.

Job descriptions govern Indian office life. Be careful not to step on toes; even sending your own fax may ruffle feathers.

When entering a taxi in Japan, the most important person sits in the middle with an acolyte on either side.

In business negotiations, expect the representatives of a traditional Chinese firm to enter the room in order of seniority.

Communication and greetings

In Japan don't raise your voice; brash westerners are perceived to be intimidating and gauche. Speak slightly more slowly than you would normally do, but not obviously so. Similarly, strong handshakes are considered aggressive.

Falling asleep in meetings or presentations is not uncommon in China and Japan. Closed eyes can also be a sign of concentration. Periods of silence during meetings and conversations are considered useful rather than uncomfortable.

Closed eyes can be a sign of concentration

In Thailand, a simple bow of the head is preferable to a handshake. The traditional "wai" (hands in prayer position while bowing) is best avoided for fear of breaching the rules of etiquette.

In London, the woes of public transport are a sure-fire way of reviving flagging conversation.

business etiquette tips *continued*

Like many Germans,
Berliners tend to be earnest
and straightforward. It is best
to say exactly what you mean

> **❝ keep attempts at humour out of business meetings ❞**

and to keep attempts at humour out of business meetings.
Irony can be taken the wrong way.

In keeping with their political system, the Swiss are
experts at consensus building, and will happily debate an
issue until all parties are satisfied.

Good manners mean that a Mexican will sometimes be
evasive to avoid disappointing. "Maybe", "probably", "I
think so", and "I'll have to check" often mean "no".

Your Russian counterparts may insist that they
understand something, when this is not actually the case.
Moreover, they sometimes have a tendency to say things
they think you want to hear.

If doing business in France, remain polite and cordial
during a first meeting and keep in mind that the French
tend to be suspicious of early friendliness. Many French
consider effusive smiles to be *de trop*. A polite nod of the
head will win you more respect.

Germans are quite likely to draw attention to deficiencies
in your products or services if they do not correspond to
your claims. This is simply because they see nothing
wrong in pointing out facts.

At the end of a meeting or presentation, Germans often
signal their approval or thanks by gently rapping their
knuckles on the tabletop instead of applauding.

When bidding farewell to a group of Indian colleagues,
take time to address each person individually.

In China, *"Bu fangbian"* ("It is not convenient") is a polite way of saying that something is impossible or very difficult.

Deadlines and punctuality

In Germany and Switzerland, always try to be on time or, if possible, early to appointments, and arrange for meetings or interviews well in advance. In Spain, by contrast, do not be offended if your contact turns up 15 or 20 minutes late for a meeting.

Muslims answer the call to prayer five times a day. Long meetings in the Arab world may be interrupted accordingly.

In Japan, don't expect an immediate response to anything. Decisions are usually made collectively, and answers typically take much longer than in western companies. Once a decision is taken in Japan, however, the machine rolls forward smoothly and action is speedy.

In France, the quality of a product and the persuasiveness of an argument are far more important than the setting of deadlines.

No-nos

In Arab countries, male business travellers should not flirt with local women.

In Japan, do not leave your chopsticks standing upright in a bowl of rice: this resembles a Buddhist funerary custom.

When in Russia, don't shake hands through a doorway, light a cigarette from a candle, bring an even number of flowers, or whistle indoors.

Don't boast about your past when visiting California. Here, your pedigree counts for less than your next big idea.

business etiquette tips *continued*

In Hong Kong blinking at someone is considered impolite.

Many Singaporeans interpret strong eye contact as aggressive. In meetings, expect to see downward glances, especially from those lower in status. Pounding one fist into the palm of the other hand is a gesture to avoid as

many people perceive it to be obscene. And the "arms akimbo" position – standing tall with your hands on your hips – is typically perceived as an angry and aggressive posture.

Eating and drinking

Breakfast meetings are rare in London. Most Brits subscribe to Oscar Wilde's claim that "only dull people are interesting at breakfast".

Wolfing down a sandwich at work confirms the worst French stereotypes of Anglo-Saxons. Lunch, usually a sit-down affair, is treated as a break from the office, and conversation over food is rarely work-related. To refuse wine at a business lunch would be permissible, but to refuse it at a dinner could be considered rude.

In Russia, always hand in your coat at the cloakroom when visiting a restaurant – draping it over the back of your chair is frowned upon.

When in Italy, order an espresso after eating. Topping off a meal with a frothy cappuccino would be unthinkable to a native.

In Japan, never blow your nose on the *oshibori* (a tightly rolled hot towel).

According to German superstition, if you don't look into another person's eyes when clinking glasses, seven years of bad sex will follow.

No Russian drinks vodka without *zakuski* (snacks) or a sniff of some black bread after each shot to help soak up the alcohol.

Social drinking is common in Mexico, where you can expect a boozy lunch and possibly a visit to a strip club to celebrate closing a deal.

In New York, business lunches tend to be dominated by work matters; the focus is not on the food and drink. Smoking (now banned in all restaurants and bars) is usually seen as a sign of weakness, not sophistication. The liquid lunch is a rarity: most New Yorkers stick to sparkling mineral water.

Toasts are important in Russia. Drink to international friendship, the success of an enterprise, or any other heart-warming goal.

Personal face and space

Never underestimate the importance of "saving face" in Asia and East Asia. Causing embarrassment and loss of "face" can scupper the best-laid business plans.

Tactile displays of emotion (back slaps, hugs) and kissing on both cheeks are quite acceptable among men in Saudi Arabia and the Gulf.

Strict Muslim men will not shake hands with women they are not related to. As an alternative, press your palm lightly over your heart.

business etiquette tips *continued*

Personal space is not highly regarded in China: expect people to get quite close to you.

Conversely, public displays of affection or prolonged body contact would be inappropriate in Japan and Korea.

Sartorial tips

Italians have a tendency to notice shoes straight away – keep yours shiny and in good shape.

Women travellers should dress conservatively in the Middle East (long sleeves and skirts below the knees).

In Latin American cities, high heels, short skirts and plunging necklines are quite acceptable for women.

Shoes are not worn inside Japanese houses or temples. There will be an assortment of slippers for guests to choose from. Leave your shoes (toes pointing towards the exit) at the designated spot and enter the main room. When entering a *tatami* room, remove your slippers.

In informal Israel, do not be surprised to see executives in sandals.

Sports

Many Germans consider chat about sport the preserve of the uneducated.

But in sports-mad Australia, it helps to know who recently won the big boat racing, rugby league football and cricket matches.

Before your business meetings in South Africa, brush up on the latest triumph or failure of the Springboks.

Football (soccer) is also increasingly talked about as the country prepares to host the 2010 World Cup.

Yes and no

In Bulgaria and parts of Greece and Turkey, nodding and shaking the head have the opposite meanings they do in the rest of the world.

The Japanese avoid saying "no". "Yes" (*hai*) generally means "Yes, I hear what you are saying".

Indians and Singaporeans also dislike saying "no". Body language will often provide more clues than what is actually said. Phrase your questions to avoid a yes/no reply.

Yes = No = ?

❝ Some regard private enterprise as if it were a predatory tiger to be shot. Others look upon it as a cow that they can milk. Only a handful see it for what it really is – the strong horse that pulls the whole cart ❞

Winston Churchill,
British statesman

❝ The chief business of the American people is business ❞

Calvin Coolidge,
former American president